Prose of
Relevance 2

Kenneth J. Weber

Assistant Professor of English
Ontario College of Education

Consultant
Homer Hogan
Associate Professor of English
University of Guelph

Methuen

Toronto   London
Sydney Wellington

Library of Congress Catalog Card Number 70-146698

SBN 0-458-90700-6

Interior design by Don Kennedy

Printed and bound in Canada

75 74   4 5

Table of Contents

A Note to Teachers

Why an Oral Program?

Of all the different aspects of teaching that make up an English program *speech* must surely be the most important, for inability to speak fluently is a far worse handicap in life than inability to read or write.

Because the significant majority of all human communication is *oral,* there is obvious value in a program in speech. Whether one calls it *oral arts* or *speech arts* or *oral communication,* or any other term, the need for competence in this field is a vital one. Personal development and social competence depend to a large degree on being articulate. Human interplay hinges on clear, effective expression. (How often do we teachers, consciously or unconsciously form our impressions of students on their ability to express themselves?) In an oral program, thinking and logic come into play, helping students to develop confidence in themselves. The skills of listening and perceiving are also given their due. Discussion too, leads to writing, to improvised drama, and, of course, to language study. In the English classroom, the language environment is necessarily enriched, and there is no better place to put into force John Dixon's statement: "Language is learned in operation, not in dummy runs."

An Oral Program

Prose of Relevance presents the two primary requisites of an oral program, namely: that students must want to discuss something; and, that they must have something to discuss. Accordingly, the passages are chosen from a broad range of topics that are interesting and, of course, relevant. Each selection is designed to provide a common experience from which discussion will flow, to form a sharp focus — an outside authority — for both teacher and student. Questions are included after each article precisely because the purpose of the article is to promote investigation and discussion. A teacher can keep the response open, but when the talk grows vague or dies out, he can always return to the text.

Other Uses for Prose of Relevance

Writing: The same principles of wanting to discuss and having something to discuss, flow naturally into a writing program. Students who are moved to discuss something will write better, if only because they care about what they are doing. Many suggestions for writing have been included in *Prose of Relevance* to capitalize on this factor.

Listening: People often tend to be labelled as unintelligent, or unaware, simply because of their unwillingness or inability to listen. An oral program based on subjects of interest necessarily involves careful listening. *Prose of Relevance* includes many passages that are ideal for practice in listening for detail, and for practice in "filter-listening" — sifting out propaganda techniques. (See Appendix: The Art of Listening.)

Perceiving: Some of the articles in *Prose of Relevance* were selected deliberately because of their "leaps of logic" and questionable conclusions. In dealing with these passages, students can develop their own perception, as well as learn to view critically the strange sense of authority that print lends to a subject.

Reading: Aside from physical handicaps, most students who *want* to read, *will* read, in spite of any "reading level stigma." The inherent interest of many topics in *Prose of Relevance* utilizes this factor. (Try your students who "won't read" or "can't read" on some of the passages in "The Unexplained" from *Prose of Relevance 1* or on the opening passage of "The Trouble with Women" from *Prose of Relevance 2,* and test them for comprehension and perception.)

Drama: Several passages invite dramatic commentary. Others suggest scripting for radio or TV.

Debating and Formal Presentations: Although the formal aspect of an oral program usually plays only a minor role, many areas of the book present opportunities for debates and prepared addresses.

Prose of Relevance 1

Prose of Relevance 1, the companion volume of *Prose of Relevance 2,* contains the following chapters:

A final note:

Prose of Relevance 2 and its companion, *Prose of Relevance 1,* represent several years of collecting, sifting, and classroom testing. Like any other teacher, I have discarded over ninety per cent of the material I've used. The resulting books contain the best of what remains.

Ken Weber

Acknowledgements

Are You A Mere Sex Object? If Not, Do You Know Anybody Who Is? From *Glamour Magazine*; copyright © 1969 by The Condé Nast Publications Ltd.

What Are Women To Do? by Sylvia Sylvie. Reprinted from *The Telegram*.

No, Nu, Na, Knee, by Erma Bombeck. © 1969 Newsday, Inc. Reprinted by permission.

Men Worse Than Animals? From *The Human Zoo* by Desmond Morris. By permission of Jonathan Cape Ltd. and The McGraw-Hill Book Company.

The Trenches In World War I. From *In Flanders Fields* by Leon Wolff. Reprinted by permission of The Longman Group Limited and The Viking Press.

The Old Soldier Didn't Like To Kill, But The New GI Does It With Ease, by William Braden. By permission of *The Chicago Sun Times*.

The Pinkville Terror. Reprinted from *The Telegram*.

How Dare You Tell A Child He's Lucky To Be Alive? By permission of the Associated Press.

Waging War The Modern Way © 1969 by The New York Times Company. Reprinted by permission.

Cheap H-bomb for any nation, General warns, by Harold King. Reprinted from *The Telegram*.

Your Attention Please. From *Once Bitter, Twice Bitter,* by Peter Porter, Scorpion Press.

The Problem; Why Has The Problem Become A Crisis?; and How Did We Get Into Such Trouble? From *The Population Bomb.* Copyright © 1968 by Paul R. Ehrlich. Published by Ballantine Books, Inc.

Food Raids By Brazil Peasants. By permission of Reuters.

Judy. Reprinted from *The Telegram*.

"I Am A Drug Addict": An Autobiography. © 1968 by The New York Times Company. Reprinted by permission.

Drugs And The Law; Drugs As A Part Of Culture; and Chasing The Weed. From *Drugs & The Law,* by Reginald Whitaker. © 1969 by Methuen Publications.

To Hunt Or Not To Hunt. From *They Call It Sport,* by James McAree. Reprinted from *The Globe and Mail.*

All In The Cause of Good Fellowship. From *Shooting An Elephant* by George Orwell. Copyright 1945, 1946, 1949, 1950, by Sonia Brownell Orwell. Reprinted by permission of Harcourt Brace Jovanovich, Inc. and A. M. Heath & Company Ltd.

Why They Won't Fight, by William Spenser. Reprinted from *Weekend Magazine.*

Conscience For Change, by Martin Luther King. Copyright © Martin Luther King Jr., 1967. *CBC Massey Lectures.* CBC Publications, Toronto, and by permission of Hodder and Stoughton Ltd. and Harper & Row Inc.

Survival Kit. Reprinted from *RAT Magazine.*

Canada: A Haven For Cowards. Reprinted from *Weekend Magazine.*

"The remarkable phenomenon . . ." by Daniel Cohn-Bendit. From *Obsolete Communism: The Leftwing Alternative* by Daniel and Gabriel Cohn-Bendit. Reprinted by permission of André Deutsch and The McGraw-Hill Book Company.

Why Christians And Atheists Find They Have A Great Deal In Common, by Wayne Edmondstone. Reprinted from *The Toronto Daily Star.*

Religion And World History, by W. W. Bauer. By permission of the author.

Religion Is The Extra Dimension, by Most Rev. Philip Hannan; **Tradition And Meaning,** by Chaim Potok; and **The New-Time Religion,** by Rev. Robert Raines. Reprinted from *Ladies' Home Journal* by permission of Transworld Feature Syndicate Inc.

The Twenty-fifth of December, by Raymond Souster. Reprinted from *The Colour of the Times,* by Raymond Souster, by permission of The Ryerson Press, Toronto.

God Is For Real, Man, by Rev. Carl Burke. From *God Is For Real, Man,* by Rev. Carl Burke.

Reprinted by permission of Association Press and Collins Publishers.

Today's Youth, by Kenneth Keniston. From *Youth Change and Violence,* by Kenneth Keniston. Reprinted by permission of the author.

Telling Lies To The Young Is Wrong, by Yevgeny Yevtushenko, translated by Robin Milner-Gulland and Peter Levi, S.J. Reprinted by permission of Penguin Books Ltd.

The Gap, by Lorber and Fladell. From *The Gap,* by Lorber and Fladell. Reprinted by permission of The McGraw-Hill Book Company and Barrie & Jenkins Inc.

The Trouble With Parents, by Sylvie Reice. From the September 1969 issue of *McCall's.* Reprinted by permission of *McCall's Magazine.*

Between Parent And Teenager, by H. Ginott. Reprinted from *The Telegram.*

Why They Leave Home, by Rev. Larry Beggs. From *Huckleberries for Runaways.* Ballantine Books.

The Young Re-reviving Ancient Communal Living, by Trent Frayne. Reprinted from *The Toronto Daily Star.*

I've Had It Up To Here With The Youth Cult, by Oliver Clausen. Reprinted from *The Globe and Mail.*

Judge Bans Child Auction. Reprinted by permission of United Press International.

Spent 34 years in jail for $5 candy theft, He asks compensation. Reprinted by permission of Associated Press.

Millionaire tried in closed court. Reprinted from *The Telegram.*

The Future For The Law, by John Turner. Reprinted by permission of the author.

Stay In School — The Magnificent Obsession, by Walter Pitman. By permission of the author.

What Is Education For? From *Living and Learning.* By permission of the Ontario Department of Education.

The Way It Spozed To Be, by J. Herndon. Copyright © 1965, 1968 by the author. Reprinted by permission of Simon & Schuster Inc.

The New York City Student Code. From *Practical English.* Reprinted by permission of Scholastic Magazines, Inc.

Eco-Catastrophe, by Dr. Paul Erlich. Reprinted by permission of the author.

Select Samaritan, by Robert Finch. Reprinted from *Poems* by Robert Finch by permission of Oxford University Press (Canadian Branch).

Is The Answer In "Black Power"? By permission of the United States National Advisory Commission on Civil Disorders.

Black Power: Two Views — from *What We Want,* by Stokely Carmichael. By permission, the Student Non-Violent Co-ordinating Committee; and from the testimony of Roy Wilkins before a United States Senate committee investigating civil disorders.

The Way of The Indian. From *The Way of the Indian,* CBC Publications. Copyright © Canadian Broadcasting Corporation 1961.

Government May Take Action Against A Band of Cree Indians. Reprinted by permission of Canadian Press.

Polish Anti-Semitism Sparks An Exodus to Denmark. Reprinted by permission of The Los Angeles Times/Washington Post News Service.

NAACP Advertisement. Courtesy NAACP Special Contribution Fund.

Photos and Illustrations

The New York Times — p. 117.
Radio Times Hulton Picture Library — p. 215.
Lawrence Fried — p. 157.
The Globe and Mail — p. 147.
United Press International — p. 58.
Ontario Water Resources Commission — p. 190.
The Harbinger — pp. 31-32.
National Film Board — pp. 172, 182.
Miller Services — pp. 221, 223.
The Telegram — pp. 95, 195, 210.
Wheeler Newspaper Syndicate — pp. 19, 34, 218.
The Toronto Daily Star — pp. 4, 74, 93, 115, 122, 134, 198, 199.

1. THE TROUBLE WITH WOMEN

The average adult male's brain weighs 3 pounds, 1.73 ounces. The average adult female's brain weighs 2 pounds, 12.83 ounces.

Woman's Place

from the 1800-1810 edition of the Encyclopaedia Britannica

The man, more robust, is fitted for severe labour, and for field exercise; the woman, more delicate, is fitted for sedentary occupations, and particularly for nursing children. The man, bold and vigorous, is qualified for being a protector; the woman, delicate, and timid, requires protection. Hence it is that a man never admires a woman for possessing bodily strength or personal courage; and women always despise men who are totally destitute of these qualities. The man, as a protector, is directed by nature to govern; the woman, conscious of inferiority, is disposed to obey. Their intellectual powers correspond to the destination of nature. Men have penetration and solid judgment to fit them for governing, women have sufficient understanding to make a decent figure under a good government; a greater portion would excite dangerous rivalry between the sexes, which nature has avoided by giving them different talents. Women have more imagination and sensibility than men which make all their enjoyments more exquisite; at the same time that they are better qualified to communicate enjoyment. Add another capital difference of disposition: The gentle and insinuating manners of the female sex tend to soften the roughness of the other sex; and wherever women are indulged with any freedom, they polish sooner than men.

These are not the only particulars that distinguish the sexes. With respect to the ultimate end of love, it is the privilege of the male, as superior and protector, to make a choice; the female preferred has no privilege but barely to consent or to refuse . . . Among all nations it is the practice for men to court, and for women to be courted; and were the most beautiful woman on earth to invert this practice, she would forfeit the esteem, however by her external grace she might excite the desire, of the man whom she addressed. The great moral virtues which may be comprehended under the general term integrity are all absolutely necessary to make either men or women estimable; but to procure esteem to the female character, the modesty peculiar to their sex is a very essential circumstance. Nature hath provided them with it as a defence against the artful solicitations of the other sex before marriage, and also as a support of conjugal fidelity.

1. Does this selection describe what *is*, or what it feels *should be?*
2. Which of the facts and attitudes of 1800 have changed in just under 200 years?
3. ". . . wherever women are indulged with any freedom, they polish sooner than men." (end of first paragraph) Is that statement true today?

Most women have no characters at all. (Alexander Pope, poet, 1735.)

*   *   *

. . . we should regard the female nature as afflicted with a natural defectiveness. (Aristotle, philosopher, c. 332 B.C.)

*   *   *

Dissimulation is innate in women . . . (Schopenauer, philosopher, c. 1850)

*   *   *

We have medicines to make women speak; we have none to make them keep silence. (Anatole France, writer, 1912)

*   *   *

Women then, are only children of a larger growth. (Lord Chesterfield, 1748)

*   *   *

Women and elephants never forget an injury. (Saki [H. H. Munro], writer, 1904)

*   *   *

Three things have been difficult to tame—the ocean, fools, and women. We may soon be able to tame the ocean; fools and women will take a little longer. (Spiro T. Agnew, politician, 1969)

4. Why do women cause statements like these?

Are You A Mere Sex Object? If Not, Do You Know Anybody Who Is?

from an editorial in Glamour Magazine

Every time we begin to think that the subject of women as a special interest group—their nature, assets, liabilities, and conditions of servitude—has been mercifully laid to rest, something else happens.

This time a Canadian anthropologist with the delightful name of Lionel Tiger has written a book called *Men in Groups* in which he tells us that, because of their biological nature, men since prehistory have banded together in groups to deal with the affairs of the world. Women, on the other hand, because of their biological natures, have attached themselves to individual men and not banded together at all, which is why women have never made much of a mark as generals, statesmen or corporation presidents.

Surpisingly—or not surprisingly—the women's liberation groups support Mr. Tiger's findings. Men have, indeed, always banded together in groups. But not, according to the ladies, with the purpose of dealing effectively with the world. They do it to keep women in bondage, to keep them in what the liberation calls the degrading roles of wives and childbearers, if not courtesans and prostitutes. Women, therefore, have been forced to assume these roles in order to survive and to wear the badges of their shame—cosmetics, spike heels, false eyelashes and the like—in order to ensnare men who regard them as mere sex objects.

But feminists are doing things to change this. They learn karate, the better to straighten men out. To change the sex object image they burn their bras, scorn cosmetics, dress with careful plainness. Marriage is out. Babies are OK, but fathers stay away. They discuss quite seriously the merits of an all-female society, to the point of debating whether it is ultimately better to kill off all the men or simply to keep them in zoos.

There are plenty of analysts of our changing society who believe that women now have the advantage. We are moving into a world where feminine co-operativeness, imagination, ability to deal with people and achieve ends by means of persuasion, not muscle, are the needed qualities. In the new society these same traits make women better able than men to function in the world at large. Which makes the introduction of the killer female of the liberation movement at this point a tiny bit redundant.

The women's liberation movement may, however, be liberating us from something, and that is the dutiful lip-service we seem to pay to all the women's rights movements without quite knowing why we do so. If all that these girls can wring out of women's rights is women's wrongs, if all this concentrated female energy in search of something meaningful to protest can't come up with anything better than girdles or getting whistled at in the street, if their idea of solving social problems is fantasies of killing off men—there's a message in it. Which is, it is later than you think. Women are in better shape than most of us realize.

There are still laws and employment practices that need revising. We could certainly use some tax adjustments and day-care centres. There are still some treaties to sign, negotiating to do and loose ends to tie up. But the war between men and women has been over for a long, long time.

5. Who do you think wrote this: a man or a woman?
6. Examine carefully some magazines like *Glamour, Ingenue, Seventeen, Cosmopolitan, Ladies Home Journal, Chatelaine.* Does each magazine contribute to feminism or to the image that feminism deplores?

What Are Women To Do?

by Sylvia Sylvie

In the United States the President's Commission on the Status of Women surveyed the communications industry in an attempt to discover how women were portrayed by the mass media. Here is a sampling of what they were told:

Bennett Korn (with an independent television company) noted that women are presented in an unrealistic way. "They seem to be typically in the middle-income groups, subservient to the male who earns the money. Women are never portrayed as a serious partner or breadwinner. You never see creative women in politics or as working mothers." (Except Julia and Lucy.)

Playwright Lorraine Hansberry added that the image of women frequently portrayed is "the glorification of the courtesan, the notion of women as objects and very little else." The uniform, shallow, even grotesque image in commercials, she felt, plays a part in determining standards of womanhood for the younger generation.

Writer Marya Mannes, while agreeing with Miss Hansberry's viewpoint, took exception to the word "courtesan." She felt it was the "bunny" and the entire Playboy psychology that were degrading to women.

Cartoonist Al Capp, in defending the woman in the commercial as an ideal, cited the value to American women of having as an ideal "an impossibly attractive, charming, cultured woman, and all the girls in the country trying to be like her. There's not a woman in this room who hasn't been influenced by this means," he told the commission.

For the educated housewife there are three traditional alternatives to the career that might have been. There is, according to Talcott Parsons, "the feminine glamor pattern to offset the masculine occupational status and its attendant symbols of prestige."

DISADVANTAGE

This is the "Dolly Madison syndrome," where the woman devotes her time to making herself physically attractive and expensively and elaborately dressed. The built-in disadvantage is that it becomes increasingly more challenging as the years pass and the wrinkles appear.

Then there is the "Jackie Kennedy syndrome" where the woman decides to acquire a mature appreciation and systematic cultivation of cultural interests and educated tastes—extending all the way from the intellectual sphere to art, music and household furnishings.

Finally, there is the "Eleanor Roosevelt syndrome" where the woman plunges into humanitarian works in the community, becoming involved with underprivileged children, the cancer fund, slum clearance.

Says Dr. Parsons: "Marriage is the 'single event' in a woman's life. It is marriage that determines a woman's fundamental status. After that her role patterning is not so much status-determining as a matter of living up to expectations and finding satisfying interests and activities . . .

"The strain is added to by the lack of a clear-cut definition of the adult feminine role. Once the element of career has been eliminated, there tends to be a rather unstable oscillation between emphasis in the direction of domesticity, or glamour, or good companionship."

He concludes that such a situation "is likely to produce a rather high level of insecurity."

Margaret Mead has talked about the necessity of developing an attitude of "mutual responsibility" between the sexes. By this she means, "creating a world in which men's and women's gifts are used mutually, in all their great similarity, in all their possible deep differences, to build a world in which no human gift is disallowed because there are not cultural forms through which it can be expressed."

Most people would agree that such a world is still a long distance away.

*   *   *

7a. Does marriage cause problems for women?
  b. Does the article advocate careers or marriage for women?

8. In your opinion, are women biologically oriented to the kind of fulfilment outlined in this article?

9. In the 1960's, both Canada and the United States held commissions investigating the status of women. Why has this become such a concern in *western society* and in the *twentieth century*?

... a female is something deficient and by chance.

Saint Thomas Aquinas

No, Nu, Na, Knee

by Erma Bombeck

Margaret Mead, the anthropologist, is predicting that within a few years men will stay home to mind the children while the mothers go out to work.

It all started, she says, during the middle 1940's when men baby-sat their own children and went to postwar night school while their wives assumed the burden of family support.

According to Dr. Mead, "This will constitute a sexual breakdown." (That's not the only breakdown they'll experience.) Raising kids is not a Minnie Mouse job for amateurs.

First, you have to be able to communicate with your toddlers. We all know when baby says, "No, nu, na, knee" and tops it off with a saliva bubble he is saying, "Daddy." But what about the other translations that are not so simple to unscramble?

For example, a small child will have 50 or 60 expressions to indicate when he has to use the bathroom. I have been around children who have used such descriptive words as "tinkle, toi toi, potty, john john, head head, can can, stinko and wee wee. (The latter is not to be confused with wa wa which is either a cold drink of water or a French horn, depending on the maturity of the child.)

Fathers will also learn children will spend as much as five or six daylight hours standing in front of a kitchen cupboard flexing their fist in and out crying, "baja . . . baja . . . baja."

Now what is baja, you might ask. Good question. Only the child knows for sure, so with painstaking thoroughness you must go through the spices, staples, glassware, bar supplies, cleaning cans, china and small appliances. It is only through a stroke of luck that you discover baja is a yellow crayon that rolled under the freezer. (On some occasions baja has meant he wants the can of chili powder he was sucking on until someone took it away from him.)

The only thing you can count on in a child's vocabulary is that when he says, No, he means No! Other than that you have to take one word at a time.

Uncle Dodo is Aunt Mildred. Muck is milk. Ghaspetti is pizza with everything except anchovies. Doggie is a cat, horse, pig, goat or chicken. Bow Wow is a dog. Daddy is anyone in long pants including Uncle Dodo in slacks.

I can't see fathers spending an entire day with a kid who follows him around whining, "Daddy, voola, Daddy, voola." (Which means "Blow up my balloon or I'll suck myself up the sweeper nozzle.")

Child raising is a tough racket. You have to break the "code" before it's too late.

10. Do women have a better sense of humour than men?
11. Why are women able to manage children better than men?

O men, respect women who have borne you.

The Koran

Please Let Women Be Women Again

"If women do get what they want, it'll probably turn out with women losing all the respect from men that they ever had. And I wouldn't blame the men one bit."

So wrote a girl in Grade 12, in the teen section of a Canadian newspaper. She was criticizing the militancy of the feminist movement.

And she has a point! Women with their constant agitation for *equal* status and *equal* rights, are quite likely to destroy all the advantages of being a woman. In many ways the entire movement is a foolish one, for women have not only enjoyed protection, but *superior* status for centuries, simply because of their sex. In times of crisis men have displayed courage and resourcefulness that they didn't even know they had, in order to ensure the safety of their women. And what woman has not enjoyed the pampering, the indulgence, and the comfort given her, simply because she is a woman? What country would have launched a thousand ships to bring back a woman who wore pants, and carried placards outside the palace? What knight would mount his charger to rescue a damsel who smokes cigars and spits into the moat?

Even worse than what the feminists are doing to their own sex, is what they may do to society at large. Much of the warmth, the humanity, and the goodness in our society comes from the influence of women. What child when he is hurt, does not run to his mother for comfort? What teenager when the chips are down, does not seek solace from a mother? When a man young or old, does something worth shouting about, who is the first person he shouts it to? Who is a better companion than a wife? Who is more helpful than a kind, loving woman? It is women who have perpetuated the gracefulness and refinement that separate us from barbarism, women who inspire poets, heroes, all men, to greater things. Without women as women, the whole fabric of our civilization would crumble.

And who would fill their role if the change did come? Certainly not the feminists! As a group they are frustrated, hard, unfriendly types who have failed as women and are trying to become men. This is obvious since they do not devote their energies as much to improve the lot of women as they do to destroying what they call male domination.

Yet even the most militant of the feminists cannot agree on objectives. Some feel the male should be eliminated entirely. (Probably, if this group were successful, this is what the males would want anyway.) Others want equal status while still retaining all the advantages of womanhood. No matter which group succeeds in becoming dominant, the long range impact of feminism will not be felt as much by today's adults as by tomorrow's. It is girls who are teenagers today, who must decide whether it is worth giving up a few insignificant things, to enjoy the delights of being a woman.

12a. Would the writer of this article agree that women should be educated? What kind of education would this same person probably recommend?

b. Which term would most accurately describe the writer:
        pro-women?
        anti-feminist?
        pro-men?

THINK

(a) Resolved: That women should be kept barefoot, and at the stove.

(b) Resolved: That educating women is time and effort spent unwisely.

(c) Resolved: That working mothers are the root cause of most of the social unrest we experience today.

(d) Form panels on which both sexes are represented, and consider *objectively,* the following questions:

    i. What would be the social implications of eliminating marriage?

    ii. Does the fact that a wife must take the name of her husband, contribute to a loss of her identity?

    iii. Is it possible that women *deserve* fewer promotions, and lower salary?

    iv. Does the fact that women can have babies, make them more emotionally stable, and does this fact explain why women are less likely to "climb mountains" than men?

(e) Using a secret ballot method, poll several classes in your school, having them answer *yes* or *no* to: "According to your feelings, do women actually *want* to be equal to men?"

(f) "Teenage girls today aren't very pretty. They behave sloppily; they dress like boys; they don't act in a lady-like manner; as a matter of fact they seem to put as much effort into being as *unpretty* as their mothers did into looking pretty." Is this true?

(g) For investigation:

    i. Set up a structure for determining how advertising affects the image of women. (For example, in a heterosexually oriented magazine like *Life,* or *Maclean's,* count the number of ads. How many are directed at women? Put these ads into categories—degrading—flattering—sex objects—etc.)

    ii. Try to find out what the status of women employees is in your area.

(h) Some interesting results might come from a survey in your school. The survey would have to be adapted to the particular school you attend, but the following sample questions would have fairly universal application:

    i. Do you feel that girls and boys in the school are treated equally?

    ii. Do you want to marry before you are twenty-five?

    iii. (Boys) Do you regularly hold doors open for girls?
       (Girls) Do you regularly wait for boys to open doors for you?

2. WAR: A NATURAL STATE?

In Napoleon's victory at Austerlitz in 1805, approximately 34,000 men were lost. In the bombing of just four cities in World War II (Tokyo, Dresden, Hiroshima, and Nagasaki) the victorious Allies killed over 328,000 people. The Nazi S.S. at Dachau concentration camp alone, exterminated around 70,000 people. The city of Herat in 1232, held out for six months against the Mongols under Genghis Khan. After their victory, the Mongols took almost a week to kill every man, woman, and child. It is said that of a whole city, only forty people survived.

Men Worse Than Animals?

from The Human Zoo

by Desmond Morris

QUESTION: What is the difference between black natives slicing up a white missionary and a white mob lynching a helpless Negro?

ANSWER: Very little—and, for the victims, none at all. Whatever the reasons, whatever the excuses, whatever the motives, the basic behaviour mechanism is the same. They are both cases of members of the in-group attacking members of the out-group.

Using a harsh evolutionary argument, it might be suggested that if two groups clash and one exterminates the other, the winner is biologically more successful than the loser.

But if we view the species as a whole this argument no longer applies. It is a small view.

The bigger view is that if they had contrived to live competitively but peacefully alongside one another, the species as a whole would be that much more successful.

It is this large view that we must try to take. If it seems an obvious one, then we have some rather difficult explaining to do.

We are not a mass-spawning species like certain kinds of fish which produce thousands of young in one go, most of which are doomed to be wasted and only a few survive.

We are not quantity breeders, we are quality breeders, producing few offspring, lavishing more care and attention on them and looking after them for a longer period than any other animal.

After devoting nearly two decades of parental energy to them it is, apart from anything else, grotesquely inefficient to send them off to be knifed, shot, burned and bombed by the offspring of other men.

Yet, in little more than a single century (from 1820 to 1945) no less than 59,000,000 human animals were killed in inter-group clashes of one sort or another.

We describe these killings as men behaving "like animals," but if we could find a wild animal which showed signs of acting this way, it would be more precise to describe it as behaving like men.

The fact is that we cannot find such a creature. We are dealing with another of the dubious properties which make modern man a unique species.

INBORN TASK

Biologically speaking, man has the inborn task of defending three things: himself, his family and his tribe.

As a pair-forming, territorial, group-living primate he is driven to this, and driven hard. If he or his family or his tribe is threatened with violence, it will be all too natural for him to respond with counter-violence.

As long as there is a chance of repelling the attack, it is his biological duty to attempt to do so by any means at his disposal. For many other animals the situation is the same, but under natural conditions the amount of actual physical violence that occurs is limited.

It is usually little more than a threat of violence answered by a counter-threat of counter-violence. The more truly violent species all appear to have exterminated themselves—a lesson we should not overlook.

This sounds straightforward enough, but the last few thousand years of human history have over-burdened our evolutionary inheritance. A man is a man and a family is still a family, but a tribe is no longer a tribe. It is a super-tribe.

If we are ever to understand the unique savageries of our national, idealistic and racial conflicts we must examine the nature of this super-tribal condition.

It is a story of piling on the agony. The first important step was taken when we settled down in permanent dwellings.

This gave us a definite object to defend. Our closest relatives, the monkeys and apes, live typically in nomadic bands. Each band keeps to a general home range but constantly moves about inside it.

If two groups meet and threaten one another, there is little serious development of the incident. They simply move off and go about their business.

Once early man became more strictly territorial, the defence system had to be tightened up.

But in the early days there was so much land and so few men that there was plenty of room for all. Even when the tribes grew bigger, the weapons were still crude and primitive. The leaders were themselves much more personally involved in the conflicts.

As soon as farming man became urban man, another vital step was taken toward more savage conflict. The division of labor and the specialization which developed meant that one category of the population could be spared for full-time killing —the military was born.

With the growth of the urban super-tribes, things began to move more swiftly. Social growth became so rapid that its development in one area easily got out of phase with its progress in another.

The more stable balance-of-tribal-power was replaced by the serious instability of super-tribal inequalities.

As civilizations flourished and could afford to expand, they frequently found themselves faced, not with equal rivals who would make them think twice and indulge in the ritualized threat of bargaining and trade, but with weaker, more backward groups that could be invaded and assaulted with ease.

Flicking through the pages of an historical atlas one can see at a glance the whole sorry story of waste and inefficiency, of construction followed by destruction, only to be followed again by more construction and more destruction.

As the super-tribes became bigger and bigger, the task of ruling the sprawling, teeming populations became greater, the tensions of over-crowding grew, and the frustrations of the super-status race became more intense.

There was more and more pent-up aggression, looking for an outlet. Inter-group conflict provided it on a grand scale.

1. According to this article, to what extent is a man biologically aggressive, and to what extent does his environment make him aggressive?
2a. What do these terms mean:
   pair-forming?
   territorial?
   group-living?
 b. What distinguishes a super-tribe from a mere tribe?
3. "If the premises of this article are true, then the world will continue to have wars simply because of over-population." Do you agree?

The Trenches In World War I

from In Flanders Fields
by Leon Wolff

The stretcher-bearers first retrieved the seriously wounded British; then the moderately wounded British; then the British dead; then the German lightly wounded. The German seriously wounded mostly had to be ignored, and enemy dead in No-Man's-Land were never touched by British bearers except for souvenirs. While on an individual basis the campaign was fought by both armies with reasonable decency, sometimes hideously wounded men found lying on the battlefield were mercifully shot by their opponents. In one reported instance a British officer scouting the area came across an enemy soldier mangled but still alive. 'Shoot him,' he said unhappily to his runner, as the German lay watching them in a stupor of agony. The runner unslung his rifle but could not fire, nor could another soldier in the little patrol. The officer drew his own pistol, stared in gloom at the German writhing on the ground below; and could do no more. Later he said savagely; 'Damn funny, wasn't it? And we just left him there, so I suppose he'll die in the mud tonight.'

One photograph shows six stretcher-bearers carrying one wounded soldier back from the front. The bearers, up to mud from one's ankles to another's hips, seem to be smiling almost apologetically. All day the walking wounded in their bandages drifted back, punctured and lacerated in the usual ways of war, trudging along the porridge-like roads in their heavy boots which resembled nothing but blobs of mud. (Some got lost at night and walked the wrong way—directly back into the wire.) At regimental-aid posts, only a few hundred feet rearward, doctors worked swiftly at routine first-aid or serious amputations required on the spot. Then the men were passed back to another dressing station, except for those still needing surgery, who were moved to a Casualty Clearing Station. At these collecting points the ambulances lined up by the hundreds like taxis at the Waldorf—waiting and loading and rattling through the area all day and night with their sodden cargoes. The men moaned or lay half stunned during the clattery ride back to hospital, where they would variously find peace or permanent disability, or an anti-climactic death after all.

But many of the lightly wounded were more cheerful, and joked about small injuries which meant a soft life for months, perhaps a permanent assignment in 'Blighty'. Unlike these gay chaps were the majority of silent, brooding ones who sat covered with whitish clay, staring at charcoal stoves and waiting for ambulances. In some the spirit of soldiery sometimes still flickered, and at least one remarked sullenly, 'Only the mud beat us. We should have gone much further except for the mud.'

At the roadside dressing stations danger was not yet past, for still the Germans probed the roads and intersections with their long-range guns. Doctors themselves were killed there, and the wounded were sometimes wounded again, or finally finished off for good. At these collecting points around Broodseinde, Poelcapelle, along the Menin Road and beside the Ypres-Staden railway, the wounded congregated crying and moaning so that the sound rang in everyone's ears all day and destroyed many an appetite. And later in the day and evening some of the dead began to be hauled back in mummy-like blankets ready for burial. Pitifully small they seemed, hardly half the size of the cursing, burly fellows (four per corpse) that slid and stumbled down the tracks with their tolerant burdens.

In No-Man's-Land the wounded still lay in the mud. Their shouting and sobbing kept everyone's nerves on edge. Those in shellholes generally drowned there. Slowly they slipped down the muddy banks into the water below, too weak to hold themselves up. Their feeble whispers often could not be heard by comrades passing by. As time went on No-Man's-Land thus became converted into a vast limbo of abandoned dead and dying. Each shellhole with blood on its water usually meant another corpse entombed below.

Unfortunately the harried stretcher-bearers had encouraged the wounded to try to make their own way back. Hundreds started off, but could not keep going. Exhausted and losing blood they crawled into shellholes, only to learn that this blunder would cost them their lives. Battlefield deaths of this kind are described by a survivor.

. . . a khaki-clad leg, three heads in a row, the rest of the bodies submerged, giving one the idea that they had used their last ounce of strength to keep their heads above the rising water. In another miniature pond, a hand still gripping a rifle is all that is visible, while its next-door neighbour is occupied by a steel helmet and half a head, the staring eyes glaring icily at the green slime which floats on the surface almost at their level.

The drier portions of the battlefield held more orthodox collections of dead: one German was pinned to the ground by a bayonet around which his hands had stiffened as he tried to withdraw it. A corporal's trousers had been blown off and his belly ripped open up to the chest. The top of a machine-gunner's head was missing, and his shoulders and gun coated with blood. One corpse was so strangely battered that nobody could understand what had happened. Many hundreds bore tiny perforations not visible beneath their uniforms. Machine-gunners lay scarcely relaxed beside their machines—hard, grim fighting men still facing the enemy British. A few were fearfully butchered by near hits of large shells. The faces of the dead everywhere were brown and aghast, their white teeth always showing.

. . . The war ended at the eleventh hour of the eleventh day of the eleventh month of 1918. It had meant nothing, solved nothing, and proved nothing; and in so doing had killed 8,538,315 men and variously wounded 21,219,452. Of

7,750,919 others taken prisoner or missing, well over a million were later presumed dead; thus the total deaths (not counting civilians) approach ten million. The moral and mental defects of the leaders of the human race had been demonstrated with some exactitude. One of them (Woodrow Wilson) later admitted that the war had been fought for business interests; another (David Lloyd George) had told a newspaperman: 'If people really knew, the war would be stopped tomorrow, but of course they don't—and can't know. The correspondents don't write and the censorship wouldn't pass the truth. The thing is horrible, and beyond human nature to bear, and I feel I cannot go on any longer with the bloody business. . . .'

But now the thing was over. After a few final shells thrown into enemy lines at eleven o'clock by cannoneers who shall be for ever nameless, an uncanny silence enveloped the Western Front. Cautiously, unbelievingly, the men raised themselves above their trenches, shellholes, and dugouts, and stared at the opposing lines. Soon they became excited, and often regrettably drunk; and, as the once-hostile armies merged, the men exchanged cigarettes, wine, embraces and souvenirs. Then came the stern, inevitable order forbidding fraternisation.

4. A veteran of the trenches in World War I suggested quite seriously that the viewing of brief films of battlefield dressing stations be made compulsory at movie theatres. Any comments?
5. "While on an individual basis the campaign was fought by both armies with reasonable decency, . . ." (first paragraph) Exactly what does that statement mean? Is it possible to fight a war with reasonable decency?
6. What are some of the techniques that Wolff uses in this passage to underline the sheer horror of war?

War alone brings up to its highest tension all human energy and puts the stamp of nobility upon the peoples who have the courage to face it.

Benito Mussolini

The Old Soldier Didn't Like To Kill But The New GI Does It With Ease

by William Braden

CHICAGO

An expert in military psychiatry believes that the American GI today is profoundly different from the GI who fought in World War II or Korea.

The difference may explain the alleged massacre of civilians in the South Vietnamese village of Song My, according to Dr. Benjamin Boshes.

"We've known for some time that we've been unlocking something in the American boy that wasn't going to be pleasant," said Dr. Boshes, chairman of the department of neurology and professor of psychiatry at the Northwestern University Medical school.

"In World War II," said Boshes, "the American boy was a person who didn't want to hurt anybody, who didn't want to kill. Now we've produced a different sort of man."

In World War II, many American soldiers would not fire their rifles in combat.

Military commanders in Viet Nam have a different problem. As a combat veteran who recently returned from that country summed it up:

"It's a question now of ammunition conservation.'

He added:

"This came out in our training at the United States army infantry school at Fort Benning, Ga.

"I remember one day a captain was lecturing to a group of us who were going to be platoon leaders. He showed us a marksmanship training film that said studies in World War II indicated only a third of the men would fire their rifles in combat, and in Korea only half the men would fire.

"He said we wouldn't have that problem in Viet Nam. He said the men would turn the switch on the M-16 to automatic and blast away at everything in sight. He told us our main problem would be getting the men to control their fire. And that's the way it happened. You had to make them stop shooting, not start."

It was in this context that Boshes discussed the alleged slaughter of helpless civilians at the village code-named Pinkville on March 16, 1968.

'I'm disturbed by the transition of the American boy," he said. "One doesn't make generalities about all American boys, of course, and most of them are still decent. But the fact is, we've created an angry generation, young people who are justifiably angry about the draft, the war, their uncertainty about their future and the whole setting in this country. And under certain circumstances this can unlock a killing orgy.

"If you put angry people in a situation where there are no civilized restraints, it's like dynamite. They explode in all directions. And if they've got something in their hand that kills, they kill. It becomes a legalized release.

"It isn't that these boys wanted to kill. But they were angry. And I'm not sure they were angry at the Viet Cong. I wouldn't be surprised if the anger was directed at us, for getting them into the war. And this is what really worries me.

"Frankly, even a year or two ago, I wasn't so concerned about what was happening in Viet Nam as I was with what will happen here when all of those angry people come back.

"I remember one night just before the invasion of southern France. I was sitting with a British colonel, and he said:

'I have under my command a group of the most sophisticated killers you've ever seen. They've been trained to kill every possibly way. And may God forgive me, I hope after they accomplish their mission every man jack of them dies honorably in combat. Because if they get back to England, I don't know what will happen.'

"And now a boy killing a group of villagers. He isn't angry at these villagers; he's just angry. He's upset inside. And if he's given an order to kill, he kills everything in sight.

"I don't think it's going to stop in Pinkville. You've got the danger of it happening back here. You're bringing back angry people, and the grave danger of Pinkville is the returning veteran. You're bringing back an angry boy, quite different from a World War II veteran."

Dr. Albert J. Glass, former chief psychiatrist for the army, said that Pinkville in his opinion represents a new phenomenon.

Glass is now director of the Oklahoma department of mental health. From 1956 to 1961 he was chief consultant in psychiatry and neurology to the office of the U.S. army surgeon-general.

"I was a career regular army psychiatrist until 1963," said Glass, "and this really is unique to my experience. I never heard of anything like it in World War II or Korea.

"We'd have individuals who'd blow up and do something like this, a few people maybe, acting on their own. But never an organized group, like a company or a platoon. And that's what puzzles me, that a whole group would do this now.

"It's especially puzzling insofar as psychiatric casualties have been relatively low in this war, in spite of the ambiguous nature of the war. And I think that's significant when you talk about people 'going crazy' at Pinkville. The fact that the frequency of psychiatric problems has been less in this war makes the incident that much harder to understand."

Glass rejected the idea that the incident was racial in nature, that the American soldiers regarded the villagers as subhuman "gooks" whose lives were not important.

"That's too easy a leap psychologically," he said. "The idea that you call people by certain names doesn't mean that you really think they aren't human.

"That same term was used in Korea, and from my experience there I never regarded it as a critical factor."

The same line of thought was endorsed by the veteran quoted earlier, formerly a first lieutenant, who prefers to be anonymous.

"Our contempt was not for the enemy or people we thought might be the enemy," he said. "Our contempt was for our allies, the ARVN (South Vietnamese Army). And they're the ones we called gooks. We respected the enemy. We called him Charlie."

Sociologist H. W. Mattick, co-director of the Centre for Studies in Criminal Justice at the University of Chicago law school, said:

"In our society today there is increasingly a narrow concentration on means toward given ends, like objectives in battles or reaching production quotas or dominating a market area, with no respect for the value of truth. And a soldier in a chain of command situation is especially subjected to this and deprived of the larger picture."

"I'd agree with that," said Dr. Lewis Kurke, a former military psychiatrist who is now a zone director of the Illinois department of mental health.

"In a civilian situation," said Kurke, "we have all kinds of information input coming in to us. We judge orders and instructions that are given to us in terms of other input we get. But the input of a soldier in a combat zone is very restrictive. He has no way to judge whether what his lieutenant tells him is right and true. . . .

"Pinkville has been described as in some way sick or ill behavior. I think it probably has more to do with the peculiarities of this new kind of warfare we're in. . . .

"The definition these men had was: 'This is a village that sheltered North Vietnamese soldiers who'd been shelling our people. They are enemies, apt to kill us, and we must kill them.' So I think it's all too easy to understand how in a conflict of this sort the easy thing to do at the moment is to obey. The whole army is organized so you will react to the order.

"I think the justification was very similar in the case of

the Nazi murders in the caves of northern Italy. This town had harbored people who killed German soldiers, so they were the enemy.

"But in our army at least, you are not to obey an illegal order, which I think this clearly was. So you cannot be completely exonerated of responsibility. And I think the best support for that are the statements the men made themselves. This one man felt it was just punishment he had his foot blown off the next day.

"On the other hand, one of the great dangers we frequently get into, and are into now, is somehow holding the military at arm's length. 'They're not us. They're the army, and it's unfortunate.'

"Well, the army is us. They're our people, embedded in our culture. We define who they fight, and they're stuck with the dirty job of doing it."

---

7. In your opinion, what answer does the article imply for each of these questions:
   a. Is the military a part of the society from which it comes, or is it a separate entity?
   b. Who is at fault when a massacre of civilians takes place?
   c. Are civilian killings and other "incidents" of this type, a natural outgrowth of organized armed force?
8. What would *you* do if you were given what you felt was an "illegal" order?
9. Assuming the fact that a war is going on, is there any alternative to training soldiers to be killers?

In November 1864, the United States cavalry
attacked a Cheyenne Indian village at Sand Creek,
Colorado. The Indians raised the American flag
and a flag of truce but the attack went ahead. The
cavalry killed over five hundred Indians, more
than half of whom were women and children.

The "Pinkville" Terror

*In March 1968, an undetermined number of Vietnamese civilians
were alleged to have been shot in cold blood by American troops in
the village of May Lai (known by the troops as "Pinkville"). The
following selection is taken from newspapers at the time the incident was made public.*

WASHINGTON—A young woman standing up begging, her
children around her, knowing she would be killed an instant later.

Mangled bodies of children.

Civilians who had been killed at close range with massive open
wounds.

These were the scenes which filled U.S. lawmakers with horror
yesterday when they saw color slides of the alleged "Pinkville
massacre."

The photographs were so gruesome that Rep. Leslie Arends left
midway through the session because "I got a queasy stomach."

Senator Stephen Young described the alleged May Lai (also
known as Song My) incident as "an act of brutality that cannot have
been exceeded in Hitler's time." He said the number of slain civilians could reach 700, although he gave no source for his figures.

Rep. Arends said the pictures showed masses of bodies but did
not show that Americans did the killing.

Top army officials gave shocked members of the House of Representatives and the Senate armed services committee the most detailed accounting yet of the incident.

President Nixon, speaking through his White House spokesman, called the alleged massacre of Vietnamese civilians by U.S. troops "abhorrent" to the American conscience.

Press secretary Ronald Ziegler, speaking for the president, said "steps will be taken to assure that the illegal and immoral conduct as alleged 'will be dealt with.' "

A censored transcript of Army Secretary Stanley Resor's testimony on Capitol Hill was released after the closed-door session.

He said: "It is difficult to convey the feelings of shock and dismay which I and other civilian and military leaders of the army have experienced as the tragedy of May Lai has gradually unfolded before us."

Senator Richard Schweiker said he is convinced there was a "premeditated cover-up of this incident."

He added, however, that he thought "the cover-up doesn't get to the top leadership in Vietnam. It does go fairly high up in the chain of command in the field structure."

Senator Stephen Young said officers in Vietnam told men of the 11th Infantry Brigade who were in the May Lai area not to write to their congressmen. The senator said officers "whitewashed it," but that "murder on such a huge scale, 300 to 700 civilians cannot be whitewashed."

Rep. William Dickinson said Resor and his aides testified that between 150 and 300 Vietnamese were killed at May Lai.

Resor said the army is still investigating "the extent to which the members of Company C were acting pursuant to orders from their company commander or higher headquarters when they destroyed May Lai's buildings, and fired upon its unresisting inhabitants."

The secretary said the question of orders was one of the "critical issues" remaining to be resolved.

10a. Why is the general reaction, as reported here, so confused?
   b. Is it because the "home front" is confused and unaware that such incidents can take place?

11. If you are a citizen under legal voting age—no matter what your country—what, if any, responsibility do you bear for the situation outlined in this cartoon?

Bombs—The Indiscriminate Killers

In World War II, the German air force used terror tactics and bombed London even though much of England's military industry was outside that city. The Allies responded in kind, and in some ways took the terror tactic one step further. New techniques like fire-bombing, increased the destruction and loss of human life in German cities. The bombing of the city of Dresden, one of the Allies' most questionable decisions, took place in February 1945. That city housed no military industry; it was filled with refugees; and the city was noted all over the world as a place filled with art treasurers and beautiful architecture. Shortly after the destruction of Dresden, Prime Minister Winston Churchill wrote the following to his chief-of-staff:

It seems to me that the moment has come when the question of bombing of German cities simply for the sake of increasing the terror, though under other pretexts, should be reviewed. Otherwise we shall come into control of an utterly ruined land. We shall not, for instance, be able to get housing materials out of Germany for our own needs because some temporary provision would have to be made for the Germans themselves. The destruction of Dresden remains a serious query against the conduct of Allied bombing. I am of the opinion that military objectives must henceforward be more strictly studied in our own interests rather than that of the enemy.

The Foreign Secretary has spoken to me on this subject, and I feel the need for more precise concentration upon military objectives, such as oil and communications behind the immediate battle-zone, rather than on mere acts of terror and wanton destruction, however impressive.

*   *   *

War is the supreme test of man, in which he rises to heights never approached in any other activity.

General George S. Patton

Adolf Eichmann was hanged in Tel Aviv in May 1962. He had been one of the leaders responsible for organizing the Nazi's extermination of six million Jews. He died claiming that he was still a Christian. His last words were "I had to obey the rules of war and my flag. I am ready."

12. What are the *rules* of war?
13a. "Following orders" has been the traditional response of "war criminals." What exactly is a war criminal?
   b. What is your opinion of the traditional response (*i.e.* following orders)?
14. At the time of Eichmann's trial, many people argued that killing him would serve no purpose. Do you agree or disagree?

The Case For War

There must be some underlying importance to the fact that war has been an almost constant factor of man's existence. In almost 35 centuries of recorded history, only about 230 years have been free of wars of some kind. In spite of this man has made amazing progress, and it is almost tempting to conclude that war has had much to do with this progress.

Many arguments can be marshalled in favor of war and its contribution to the development of man. In the first place, because war is a group activity, it brings men together for a common goal. Only conquest seems to be able to unite people of diverse interests. The same is true of defence. Before such unification, people in small groups were able to make only a minimal impact on their surroundings and the world at large. But united, the groups shared an overwhelming potential.

Industralization is encouraged, expanded, and developed by the demands of war. Witness the United States. Before its Civil War, it was a relatively weak, agricultural nation. But in five years, the North particularly, had mobilized its industrial energy into a force that the world recognized.

Government too is improved by war. Because of the need for organization, the lessons of the military have taught future civil governments how to plan, develop, and carry out communal activities. Even democracy has been helped by war. Much of Europe, for example, after the wars of the late nineteenth and early twentieth centuries, changed from a highly structured class society into a more democratic one. In Vietnam, large landowners lost their dominance, as peasants for the first time obtained their own land.

Conquest also produces wealth, which leads to leisure. A natural outgrowth of this, of course, is arts and culture.

Finally, the very existence of today's nation states depends on war. What nation is there today, that cannot trace its birth in war? What nation could exist today without power and the willingness to use it?

15a. Summarize the basic arguments made in favour of war in the article above.
  b. Can you argue effectively against each of the premises?
  c. Do any of the points of the argument violate the principles of logic?

War, this monster of mutual slaughter among men, will be finally eliminated by the progress of human society, and in the not too distant future too. But there is only one way to eliminate it and that is to oppose war with war, to oppose counter-revolutionary war with revolutionary war, to oppose national counter-revolutionary war with national revolutionary war and to oppose counter-revolutionary class war with revolutionary class war. . . . When human society advances to the point where classes and states are eliminated, there will be no more wars, counter-revolutionary or revolutionary, unjust or just; that will be the era of perpetual peace for mankind. Our study of the laws of revolutionary war springs from the desire to eliminate all wars; herein lies the distinction between us Communists and all the exploiting classes.

                                    Chairman Mao Tse-Tung

---

16. Does Chairman Mao's argument break down at any point?

How Dare You Tell A Child He's Lucky To Be Alive?

written shortly after the submission of Biafra to Nigeria in January 1970

LIBREVILLE, Gabon (AP) —Biafran children sang the anthem of their lost country yesterday shuffling their feet in the dust and mumbling the part that goes "Then let us die without shedding a tear."

The children, aged 2 to 12, included some of the last pitifully undernourished ones moved out as Biafra crumbled during the weekend. They raced through the song without false reverence or concern for the right key.

Adults had told them to sing it. Adults also had lined up the thin and watery-eyed and the unsteady and had given them placards to hold that read Shame on Great Britain, Our Heads Are Bloodied But Unbowed, and Long Live Our Hero Ojukwu, a reference to Lt. Gen. Odumegwu Ojukwu, the Biafran leader who fled the country.

The scene was at a hospital run by Caritas, the Roman Catholic relief organization, near Libreville. German and French doctors there have treated children airlifted out of Biafra for more than two years.

Some of the 1,800 children at the centre were moved out into a dusty clearing so they could be seen by Jacques Foccart, aide on French African affairs to President Georges Pompidou.

Mr Foccart came in a helicopter that landed in a clearing, tossing up a thick coat of dust over the young Biafrans. They responded with the national anthem.

But inside one of the low, open buildings where the children sleep there was no singing. A 9-year-old boy named Emmanuel Angoma, his body yellowed from a lack of protein and his eyes dark marbles, sat with the stillness of an old man.

When Edith Nwume, a Biafran nurse, asked him questions in Ibo, Emmanuel replied in a slow, unhappy whisper.

"Where is your mother?"

"She's at home."

"And your father?"

"He had to go away."

"What do you want to be when you grow up?"

"A teacher."

"Are you sad that Biafra lost the war?"

Miss Nwume did not translate the question. "Well, what good is it to tell some of them?" she said. "The children always played an important part. They carried water and got firewood and wanted to be soldiers. The older ones know, of course, but the younger ones, how could they understand?"

A European in the crowd remarked that the children were lucky. Miss Nwume didn't like the remark.

"How can you tell a child he's lucky to be alive?" she demanded. "Children don't think like that. They expect to be alive. It's one of their rights. How dare you tell a child he's lucky to be alive?"

While the war went on, children who recovered in Gabon or on Sao Tome were often sent back to their parents in Biafra. A newsman who travelled with an Irish priest delivering the children to their parents in tiny huts on Biafra's red dirt roads remembered the fine reunions: sometimes tears and in one case, a punch, owed and probably remembered for four months, thrown at a little brother.

Now there is a dwindling chance that some children can ever find their parents again.

A boy like Emmanuel knows the name of his village, but other smaller children who came here with their names taped with adhesive bands on their foreheads cannot remember where they came from. Records show only the name of the hospital that dispatched them. And Nigeria considers Caritas an illegal aid group.

Miss Nwume watched the children as they stood in the sun facing the chairs set up in the shade for the distinguished visitors.

17. What would *you* have said to a Biafran child?
18. When Biafra fell, Ojukwu said that his state had been starved into submission. Did relief agencies like Caritas and many others merely prolong the agony these children suffered?

Waging War The Modern Way

As revealed by Pentagon critic Congressman *Richard D. McCarthy* (D.-N.Y.), biological weapons include stockpiles of anthrax, a very serious disease; tularemia, a sometimes fatal disease known also as rabbit fever; and Q fever, an incapacitating nonlethal disease. In addition to developing existing disease strains for military purposes, researchers at Fort Detrick, the world's largest user and killer of laboratory animals—some 60,000 animals a month are "processed" at the base—engage in what is called "biological engineering." This is the application of advanced genetic techniques and procedures to create disease organisms that are best suited for military purposes.

Our chemical warfare arsenal is, perhaps, even more impressive. Three types of riot-control chemicals have been approved for military use, ranging from a standard police tear gas to Adamsite, an arsenic-laden substance that can kill. There are also stockpiles of mustard gas—a sometime killer—and an hallucinatory gas named BZ that, the army claims, induces maniacal behavior.

There are also two different varieties of nerve gas, incredibly toxic substances that kill within seconds after minute exposure; one, called GB, was derived from the gas Sarin that was developed by the Germans during World War II. By mid-1968, more than 100 billion lethal doses of GB had been produced and stored in this country, mostly at the Rocky Mountain Arsenal outside Denver. The other nerve gas is VX, 30 times as lethal as GB; .007 of a gram of VX, which can penetrate through the skin or eyeballs, is almost certainly fatal to an average-sized man. It was the army testing of nerve gas at the Dugway Proving Grounds, 80 miles southwest of Salt Lake City, that went awry in 1968 and killed more than 6,000 sheep.

In the early 1960s the army began supplying nerve-gas shells and missiles to some of its NATO allies. At one point, nerve gas was shipped to West Germany, causing heated intra-governmental protests. The weapons are still being shipped overseas and are, of course, supplied to American army units all over the world.

Congressman McCarthy has charged the Defense Department with chemical warfare in Vietnam in its use of tear gas and criticized our chemical crop destruction and jungle de-foliation program. More than $70 million worth of these chemicals were dumped on Vietnam in 1968. Although the government denies there will be any long-range ecological effects, it is generally agreed that no such assurance is possible on the evidence. In 1969 McCarthy frustrated—almost single-handedly—the planned cross-country shipment of several hundred freight cars loaded with obsolete, but deadly, gas bombs the army wanted to dispose of in the Atlantic.

Later in the year, President Nixon renounced the use of biological warfare by the United States as well as all but defensive uses of chemical warfare. This latter did not include the use of tear gas and defoliants, and Congressman McCarthy, while hailing the President's step as "a very significant thing," urged that tear gas used in conjunction with weapons that kill also be banned.

(Note: Shortly after this article was written, President Nixon moved to reduce the size and capacity of U.S. germ warfare.)

19. "An often forgotten value of germ warfare is that, because the very idea of it is so hideous to comprehend, war is made un-thinkable."
    Your comments?
20. The whole program of chemical and biological warfare in the U.S.A. has been termed an example of "colossal arrogance." In what way is it "arrogant"? Do you agree?
21. Show how the passage tries to explain the germ warfare situation in layman's terms.

. . . one dream of the hippy group is very significant: Most of the hippies are pacifists, and a few have thought their way through to a persuasive and psychologically sophisticated "peace strategy." And society at large may be more ready now to learn from that dream than it was a century or two ago; to listen to the argument for peace, not as a dream, but as a practical possibility: something to choose and use.

Martin Luther King (1967)

Cheap H-Bomb For Any Nation, General Warns

by Harold King

PARIS—The spectre of a cheap hydrogen bomb upsetting the existing nuclear equilibrium between the United States and the Soviet Union was raised here yesterday by French Air Force General Fernand Gambiez.

The time is fast approaching when an H-bomb will be within the financial grasp of any nation capable of providing itself with the necessary technicians, he wrote in the current edition of The Review of the Ministry of Defence.

General Gambiez's statement follows reports that French scientists, using what is generally regarded as the world's most powerful laser, have generated a succession of tiny thermo-nuclear explosions.

It underlines the concern of some physicists that lasers may eventually simplify the design of devastating nuclear weapons. The U.S. Atomic Energy Commission, however, holds to the line that the laser at present would be impractical for use in the detonation of an H-Bomb.

The chemical laser, Gen. Gambiez thinks, will soon be capable of setting off a bomb without the use of uranium 235 and therefore without the need for setting up large and costly uranium refining plants.

This would enable any non-nuclear nation to develop or buy a cheap laser H-Bomb and make disarmament treaties impossible to police.

22. Can a cheap H-Bomb for every nation *force* peace?

Your Attention Please

by Peter Porter

The Polar DEW has just warned that
A nuclear rocket strike of
At least one thousand megatons
Has been launched by the enemy
Directly at our major cities.
This announcement will take
Two and a quarter minutes to make.
You therefore have a further
Eight and a quarter minutes
To comply with the shelter
Requirements published in the Civil
Defence Code—section Atomic Attack.
A specially shortened Mass
Will be broadcast at the end
Of this announcement—
Protestant and Jewish services
Will begin simultaneously—
Select your wavelength immediately
According to instructions
In the Defence Code. Do not
Take well-loved pets (including birds)
Into your shelter—they will consume
Fresh air. Leave the old and bed-

ridden, you can do nothing for them.
Remember to press the sealing
Switch when everyone is in
The shelter. Set the radiation
Aerial, turn on the geiger barometer.
Turn off your Television now.
Turn off your radio immediately
The Services end. At the same time
Secure explosion plugs in the ears
Of each member of your family. Take
Down your plasma flasks. Give your children
The pills marked one and two
In the C.D. green container, then put
Them to bed. Do not break
The inside airlock seals until
The radiation All Clear shows
(Watch for the cuckoo in your
perspex panel), or your District
Touring Doctor rings your bell.

If before this, your air becomes
Exhausted or if any of your family
Is critically injured, administer
The capsules marked 'Valley Forge'
(Red pocket in No. 1 Survival Kit)
For painless death. (Catholics
Will have been instructed by their priests
What to do in this eventuality.)
This announcement is ending. Our President
Has already given orders for
Massive retaliation—it will be
Decisive. Some of us may die.
Remember, statistically
It is not likely to be you.
All flags are flying fully dressed
On Government buildings—the sun is shining.
Death is the least we have to fear.

We are all in the hands of God,
Whatever happens happens by His Will.
Now go quickly to your shelters.

THINK

(a) Resolved: That since war is an inevitable fact of life, a nation would be wiser to abandon futile efforts at peace and, like Sparta, devote all its energies to war.

(b) Resolved: That warfare in Asia, waged by Asians, is far more common than wars waged by western countries.

(c) Resolved: That if a nation is going to wage war, it is best to wage it to the fullest possible extent with every means possible, in order to bring the conflict to its quickest possible conclusion.

(d) An international police force of western nations might have intervened in the Nigerian-Biafran conflict of the 1960's and stopped it by force. Can you think of the reasons why they didn't?

(e) The observer team of Swedes, Canadians, British, and Poles is reputed to have said of the Nigeria-Biafra conflict:
"This is Africa, and we must not apply our standards to Africa." What are our standards? What are African standards? Is this a reasonable stand to take?

(f) "If we send them over there to fight, it's our duty to back them." (father of a soldier) Is he right?

(g) After World War II, the Allies tried many Germans at Nuremburg, for "war crimes."
Is "war crimes" a contradiction in terms?
What in your opinion is the justification for such trials?
Many people felt that these trials involved considerable hypocrisy on the part of the Allies. Why?

(h) Is there such a thing as:
  a "just" war?
  a "limited" war?
  "fighting for peace"?
  "overkill"?

(i) Investigate and report on:
  the Katyn Forest "incident";
  the Lidice "incident."

3. DEATH BY POPULATION

While you are reading these words, four people will have died from starvation.

Dr. Paul Erlich

The Problem

from The Population Bomb

by Dr. Paul Erlich

The battle to feed all of humanity is over. In the 1970's the world will undergo famines—hundreds of millions of people are going to starve to death in spite of any crash programs embarked upon now. At this late date nothing can prevent a substantial increase in the world death rate, although many lives could be saved through dramatic programs to "stretch" the carrying capacity of the earth by increasing food production. But these programs will only provide a stay of execution unless they are accompanied by determined and successful efforts at population control. Population control is the conscious regulation of the numbers of human beings to meet the needs, not just of individual families, but of society as a whole.

Nothing could be more misleading to our children than our present affluent society. They will inherit a totally different world, a world in which the standards, politics, and economics of the 1960's are dead.

We must take action to reverse the deterioration of our environment before population pressure permanently ruins our planet. The birth rate must be brought into balance with the death rate or mankind will breed itself into oblivion. We can no longer afford merely to treat the symptoms of the cancer of population growth; the cancer itself must be cut out. Population control is the only answer.

1. This selection is taken from a book written in the late 1960's, at a time when only a small group of people were concerned about population control. As you read this selection, what is the *current* attitude to population control in your community? In your country? What is your attitude?

Children of persons now alive will still be here when an unbearable climax has been reached.
Hugh Keenleyside (diplomat) 1966
referring to population problems.

Why Has The Problem Become A Crisis?

It has been estimated that the human population of 6000 B.C. was about five million people, taking perhaps one million years to get there from two and a half million. The population did not reach 500 million until almost 8,000 years later—about 1650 A.D. This means it doubled roughly once every thousand years or so. It reached a billion people around 1850, doubling in some 200 years. It took only 80 years or so for the next doubling, as the population reached two billion around 1930. We have not completed the next doubling to four billion yet, but we now have well over three billion people. The doubling time at present seems to be about 37 years.* Quite a reduction in doubling times: 1,000,000 years, 1,000 years, 200 years, 80 years, 37 years. Perhaps the meaning of a doubling time of around 37 years is best brought home by a theoretical exercise. Let's examine what might happen on the absurd assumption that the population continued to double every 37 years into the indefinite future.

If growth continued at that rate for about 900 years, there would be some 60,000,000,000,000,000 people on the face of the earth. Sixty million billion people. This is about 100 persons for each square yard of the Earth's surface, land and sea.

---

*Since this article was written, new figures have been produced changing the calculated doubling time to 35 years.

2. On the absurd assumption that 60 million billion people ever did live on the face of the Earth, what are some of the methods of living they would have to adopt?

The only creatures that have benefitted fully from population growth are man, lice, houseflies, and rats.

Scientist

How Did We Get Into Such Trouble?

Why is our planet suddenly faced with the possibility of its own extinction? The reasons are several. Some go back a few billion years; others go back only a few years.

Part of the answer can be found by observing animals in nature. Frogs, for example, or turtles, or fish, insure the propagation of their own kind by producing eggs in hundreds and thousands. In this way their species will survive, because, no matter how many are eaten, or how many will die while young, some of them will manage to make it through to adulthood to start the whole process over again. These animals have found that the basic key of survival is to reproduce. Man has discovered this process too. Just as it is natural for other animals to reproduce themselves, so it is also natural for man. The first cause of the population explosion, then, is a normal one—the normal urge to reproduce.

But this in itself would not cause a problem. No animal, for example, has ever threatened to overpopulate the earth as long as he was left in his natural state. (The rabbit population of Australia was a man-made crisis.) But man is different. The first difference is in the breeding cycle. Whereas animals have a specific breeding season at a specific time of year, mankind has no such thing. His season is quite literally uncontrolled. The reason for this is the fact that sex, instead of being a mere device to propogate the species, is actually a way of life. Everything man does is related, however remotely, to sex. It enters into his relationships, his art, his cars, his conversations, everything. Because sex is so involved in man's life it leads him to be a fulltime reproducer of his own kind, and because he reproduces all the time, the population is affected.

And factor builds upon factor. Fulltime reproduction in itself does not cause overpopulation. Primitive man was pretty much the same as modern man in a sexual sense; yet he did not face the problems of population. The reason was environment. Living in caves was not exactly healthy, and hunting for food was not exactly a safe, let alone a sure, thing; the odds were often on the side of the bear. Medical practice, too, left something to be desired. In many cases, a simple wound was just as effective as a death blow. But then, about 8000 years ago, the agricultural revolution changed everything. Man found that it was easier and safer to stay in one place and raise food than it was to chase it. The next step, of course, was more elaborate homes, larger societies, and security. It was this security that led to increased reproduction, and a much better chance of survival. Today, on a much larger scale, this same process is still taking place.

The ultimate step was probably taken sometime in the 1800's, when medical science began to come into its own. By the middle of the twentieth century, man had literally developed "death control." While death rates went down, birth rates went up. The result? Population crisis.

Dr. Paul Erlich describes the results of this phenomenon in his book, *The Population Bomb*:

> The power of exported death control can best be seen by an examination of the classic case of Ceylon's assault on malaria after World War II. Between 1933 and 1942 the death rate

due directly to malaria was *reported* as almost two per thousand. This rate, however, represented only a portion of the malaria deaths, as many were reported as being due to "pyrexia."[1] Indeed, in 1934-1935 a malaria epidemic may have been directly responsible for fully half of the deaths on the island. In addition, malaria, which infected a large portion of the population, made people susceptible to many other diseases. It thus contributed to the death rate indirectly as well as directly.

The introduction of DDT in 1946 brought rapid control over the mosquitoes which carry malaria. As a result, the death rate on the island was halved in less than a decade. The death rate in Ceylon in 1945 was 22. It dropped 34% between 1946 and 1947 and moved down to ten in 1954. Since the sharp postwar drop it has continued to decline and now stands at eight. Although part of the drop is doubtless due to the killing of other insects which carry disease and to other public health measures, most of it can be accounted for by the control of malaria.

Victory over malaria, yellow fever, smallpox, cholera, and other infectious diseases has been responsible for similar plunges in death rate throughout most of the UDCs.[2] In the decade 1940-1950 the death rate declined 46% in Puerto Rico, 43% in Formosa, and 23% in Jamaica. In a sample of 18 undeveloped areas the average decline in death rate between 1945 and 1950 was 24%.

---

[1]pyrexia: a type of fever.
[2]UDC—Underdeveloped country.

Finally, what makes population control such a difficult issue is the fact that we all want to live. Man is quite fragile, and after centuries of overcoming great odds against him, the urge to survive has become very strong. Every advance in medicine is hailed as a breakthrough; governments do everything in their power to prevent death by accidents; man will expend any effort and expense to free one trapped person whose life is threatened. With this kind of thinking, there is little wonder that "death control" is a popular and respected way of thinking.

But the time to act is *now*. The time has come to turn man's instinctive urge for survival to a new fact—the realization that he is not going to survive very much longer if he does not reduce his own growth factor right away.

*   *   *

3a. Outline briefly the reasons this article gives for the population explosion.
 b. Which reason, in your opinion, is the most important?
4. Would you call this article *understated,* or *factual,* or *alarmist?* Refer to specific passages to support your choice.
5a. What are some of the recent breakthroughs in "death control"?
 b. Does this article imply that such medical research should be slowed down?
6. Try to find any example of man's interference with nature which has completely upset the balance of nature. (Australia's rabbits are one example, but there are plenty more in North America.)
7. How can man best be educated to the fact that the growth factor must be reduced? Who needs the education most, Eastern or Western peoples?

Of the nearly three and one-half million people who die each year from lack of food, most are children.

Why Must We Act NOW?

Many of the scientists who devote their energies to the population crisis, worry that mankind will suffer a near, if not total, collapse by the early 1980's or late 1970's. One reason is that the world is quickly running out of food. Even with immediate action, there could still be serious famines in many of the underdeveloped countries. The statistics to support this thinking go back to approximately 1958. Until that year, most of the underdeveloped countries had been able to keep up to the population growth in food production. But after 1958, the birth rate left the food rate behind. By 1966, according to the United Nations Food and Agriculture Organization, every person on Earth had 2% less food to eat (on a world average).

The worst example of the food crisis, of course, is India, where, in the late 1960's, population was increasing at a rate of from 14 to 18 million people per year. But most of Asia, as well as large parts of Africa and Latin America, face the same dilemma as India does.

To make matters worse, hunger is not the only problem. The difficulty is made much more complex by the fact that we are killing our own planet with pollution. The percentage of fresh water in the world is very small compared to the percentage of salt water. Yet large bodies of fresh water have recently become unusable. Lake Erie, for example, is dead. In 1955, besides the benefits of fresh water itself, Lake Erie yielded 75 million pounds of fish. Today there is no fishing industry to speak of. Rivers throughout Canada and the United States are suffering the same problem, and there is increasing evidence that the other Great Lakes are going to suffer the same fate. The United States, in fact, is running out of fresh water, and some American politicians have proposed routing Canadian fresh water southward. Canadians meanwhile have been doing a good job of destroying their own environment.

Pesticides, DDT in particular, have written another chapter of destruction. And air pollution has already reached disaster proportions. Cities like London England, or Los Angeles, are demonstrating that the atmosphere can no longer tolerate the filth and fumes they give off.

For those who optimistically propose solutions like desalinating ocean water, or pioneering settlements on planets like Mars, the answers are all too gloomy. The advancements in science have been, and are now, just too slow to curb the crisis in time. The only answer is population control NOW.

8. Would you call this selection *understated, factual,* or *alarmist?* Support your choice.
9. Should Canada sell fresh water to the United States?
10. New strains of rice are proving so successful in Asian countries that even India will likely become self-sufficient because of them. Will this discovery help or hinder finding a cure for the population problem?

In 1966 only ten countries grew more food than they consumed: Argentina, Australia, Burma, Canada, France, New Zealand, Rumania, South Africa, Thailand, U.S.A.

Food Raids By Brazil Peasants

BRASILIA (Reuters)— Thousands of starving peasants are invading towns in drought-stricken northeast Brazil and breaking into stores and homes in search of food.

Official sources say about 200,000 people are on the move in the northeast, victims of a drought which has driven them from their homes in search of work as well as food.

Six freight trains have been held up and robbed of food supplies during the last week in the area around the coastal city of Fortaleza, 1,400 miles northeast of Rio de Janeiro. *(The incident described above, occurred early in 1970.)*

THINK

(a) Some people have suggested that aid to underdeveloped countries be given only to those countries that have proven their intention to control population. Is this a good idea?

(b) i. Investigate what your province or state is doing to curb pollution of the environment.

 ii. Is your province or state doing anything for or against population control?

 iii. Write to the United Nations Food and Agriculture Organization requesting information about what is being done today on a worldwide basis to control population growth.

(c) Resolved: That all aid to underdeveloped countries be halted.

(d) Is medical aid to other countries useless without adequate food and without adequate population control?

(e) In 1966, an ex-diplomat, Mr. Hugh L. Keenleyside, published a book called *International Aid: A Summary* (McClelland and Stewart). In his book, he proposed that any one of the following nine factors (or a combination of them) could possibly happen to prevent death by overpopulation. After considering all nine, write a brief outline explaining which of them you find to be the most frightening, which you feel would be the most effective in controlling population, and which you feel will most likely happen.

1. Some *natural* law which has not yet been discovered will bring into operation an automatic check on population growth.
2. A single universal catastrophe or a series of major calamities may reduce the current population.
3. A continuous state of conventional war, if waged in a sufficiently sanguinary style, might result in a stabilized population.
4. It is possible that the increasing use of radioactive substances will effectively interfere with the reproductive capacity of human beings.
5. Some wholesale system of abortion or some scheme for the deliberate killing of persons after birth may have to be introduced.
6. A widely accepted or, if necessary, a rigorously enforced policy of sterilization might offer a somewhat less drastic method of controlling the number of births.
7. A technique may be developed that will permit the transfer of human beings to some other planet in space.
8. Alternatively, beings or substances from outer space might reach Earth and either intentionally or inadvertently destroy all human life.
9. The immediate and wholesale adoption of a conscious, deliberate policy of birth control offers the only intelligent and humane method of achieving the objective of a world population adjusted to the resources of this planet.

(f) Resolved: That since some people will never accept birth control, and since others will not accept other forms of control, the best method would be to develop better management of resources.

(g) Invite representatives to your school from OXFAM, or CUSO or the Peace Corps. (If representatives cannot come, then have class members report on the activities of these groups.)

(h) Form a United Nations in your class. Each person will represent a country (preferably one of the *have* or *have-not* countries). All the representatives must have some idea of their country's population growth, birth rate, agriculture, and politics. (You can find this in Atlases, Yearbooks, Almanacs, etc.) When your General Assembly meets, debate the motion that has been proposed by Tanzania: That all the food resources in the world be shared equally by all the people in the world.

4. DRUGS

No social problem in our history has ever brought
forth more contradiction and confusion than the
concern over drug use.

psychiatrist

Three Kinds Of Teenage Users

Among young people, drug users seem to fall into three
main categories. This excludes, of course, the great number
who try it once or twice and then forget it.

Escapists:

This is the danger group. For them, turning on really means
turning off. This is the group that runs from things they can't
handle. Escapists have always been part of every society and
when drugs are not available, alcohol will usually suffice. More
than any others, these people are in serious need of phsychiatric
help. What is so alarming is the increasing number of young
people in this category. Some authorities surmise that the number of teenage escapists has always been high, and that it is
simply the availability of drugs that makes the problem so

obvious in contemporary society. Whatever the cause of escapism, one fact is sure. Skid Row used to be the property of the winos; it may soon be taken over by the heads.

Explorers:

There have always been young people who will test their endurance or courage to the utter limits. Drugs, for this group, have simply replaced hot rods and motorcycles. When adolescents grow beyond childhood amusements, and are not given adult responsibilities, they naturally become bored. Experimentation with drugs, therefore, becomes an easy step to take.

Although some of the explorers are clearly self-destructive, even suicidal, others feel that they are taking drugs to expand their inner awareness. Either way, this group is spawned by our way of life in the western hemisphere.

Rebels:

As young people become more disenchanted with the world of their parents, they tend to reject everything in it. Very often kids smoke pot simply because it is taboo. In this sense, they are not very different from their parents and grandparents, who sneaked cigarettes and guzzled beer for much the same reason.

But the rebels have more deep-seated motives. With marijuana is associated peace and communality — a rejection of the aggressive, capitalistic, war-like world of their parents. Another motive is the reaction against technology which young people view as their parents' drug — a dehumanizing drug. Inward drugs are an antidote, the rebels say, a re-humanizing rescue from technology.

These, then, are the three main groups of drug users. There are, of course, fringe followers in each of the groups, but this is a normal part of the teenage herd-instinct.

1a. For each of the groups, are drugs a means or an end?
 b. Do the writer's three categories adequately sum up the drug users, or are there more kinds of users?
2. What approach could be used to lead each group away from drugs?

Judy

A 14-year-old girl named Judy climbed into bed in her home here last week with a 12 gauge shotgun, pointed the barrel at her head, and pulled the trigger.

The unpleasant details of the suicide of the chubby Grade 9 student would have been kept a secret except for a sentence in the bloodstained note found beside her body. It said: "I suspect I'd never have done this if it weren't for grass."

Dear Class

I've nothing of great importance to tell you except that I want to thank you for a fun's year. I really enjoyed school this year + most of my thanks for that go to the kids who sit around me which is quite a lot because there was a lot of me to sit around. The reasons for my suicide had nothing to do with school scept that I knew I was going to fail Math + Science. All other reasons are personal. This is a formal invitation to any of you here who want to go to my funeral. All you do is phone my Mom + tell her.

I'm going to give you guys some advice + don't let life get you down like it did me. All of you have great times ahead of you along with bad, but the good will outweigh the bad. Some more advise — Don't take drugs that started me on my periods of depression or black moods. I suppose I'd never have done this if it weren't for grass. I luv you all + hello

a former class mate
Judy

The Danger In Marijuana

By some strange twisting of common-sense reasoning, cannabis, or marijuana is turning out to be the good guy in the world of drugs. Teenagers especially, when confronted with the facts about heroin or LSD or amphetamines, usually admit the inherent dangers in these killer-drugs. At the same time, however, they respond in defence of their developing drug sub-culture by pointing out the harmlessness of marijuana.

Probably, marijuana enjoys its somewhat ameliorated status by reflection against other drugs. The adverse effects of heroin are well-known. LSD, known to cause brain damage, has also produced significant chromosome damage in laboratory experiments. Amphetamines are outright killers, usually by causing severe cerebral hemmorhage. Solvents are killers as well, if taken for extended periods of time; police files are filled with cases of young people who have suffered brain damage because of glue sniffing. Balanced against this crude and shocking reality, the relatively harmless effects of marijuana are almost a relief. It is believed to be non-addictive, although this fact is in dispute. Its intoxicating effects are gentle, especially compared to those of alcohol. (This fact is also in dispute.) And also it is believed that marijuana does not bring about physical changes.

Yet all these claims are based on frightfully little evidence. Just as the great claim that marijuana leads to heroin use has never been fully verified, neither has the claim that marijuana is non-addictive and non-damaging. The research has not gone on long enough. We simply don't know *for sure* what will happen to a marijuana user after ten, fifteen or twenty years.

What is perhaps even more frightening is the number of myths that surround marijuana use — myths that young people believe whole-heartedly perhaps because they find them comforting. The truth is that we don't know all we should about marijuana. For all we know, we may be producing a whole spate of marijuana-using psychotics whose presence won't even become known for another twenty years!

Another problem with marijuana, no matter how harmless it may be, is the opportunity of escape it presents to its users. Increasing evidence suggests that the real marijuana users are psychologically unstable — really in need of medical care. If these users can hide within the euphoria provided by the drug, they will not be getting the care they really need.

There is great pressure to legalize marijuana. Proponents cite the legal sale of tobacco and alcohol as their strongest argument. No doubt if tobacco and alcohol were not already legally sold, we probably would not make them legal, *knowing what we now know.* Surely we have had enough mistakes already. Let's not make another one by legalizing marijuana.

3. What is the basic point about marijuana that this writer is making?
4. Why, in the author's opinion, should marijuana users be given psychiatric help?
5. Who is in the best position to decide whether marijuana should be legalized, young people or adults?

Parents aren't getting the straight facts. They don't know what's right or wrong. I say talk to the kid. He'll tell you where drugs are at.

Mrs. Ann Scace
Ontario Mental Health Assoc.

"I Am A Drug Addict": An Autobiography

MIAMI BEACH, Feb. 13 — She stood there today, in front of the nicely-dressed, healthy-looking Miami Beach Senior High School kids, and told them about dope like nobody else I've ever heard in my life. Tears came into her eyes only once. The rest of the time she described in detail the filthy life of a junkie — her own — with such sincerity that one boy collapsed.

In her neat blue suit, Florence Fisher told them things they will never hear from their parents, from the most dedicated cop, from the hardest working narcotics expert. She was talking to them from out of her own experience, and she held nothing back.

"I am a drug addict," Florrie starts. "I haven't used anything for over four years, but I am an addict and I must remember it every day as long as I live."

A student asked Florrie if she had statistics on marijuana leading to drug addiction. Florrie answered:

"Will you believe me if I tell you that I know junkies after 23 years of living in the gutter with them? Will you believe me when I tell you that I don't know any junkie who started on horse, that they all started with pot? Will you believe me when I tell you that I agree with the doctors that marijuana is not physically addictive, but that I know it is psychologically addictive?

"I don't know statistics, but I know a thousand junkies, and I tell you that they all started on marijuana. Using drugs is sheer stupidity," she said, tears coming into her eyes. "Here I am. I loused up a complete lifetime. I'm starting a new life and I'm 49."

She begged them to become "ratfinks," to inform on their sisters and brothers and friends, "to save them before it is too late."

"All I did was start with pot. At the university I fell in love and married a young guy who wasn't a professional musician, but good enough to sit in with the good bands. My husband smoked pot, and what my love did, I did. Three months after I started, I was in jail. I was naive when I went in. I knew all about dope when I came out.

"Look at me," Florrie pleads. "I'm a 50-year-old hippie. Every vein is collapsed. I must carry my stigma all my life, a card that warns the doctor he must never try to give me a shot of anything, that only the vein in my neck can be used to take blood out if necessary."

_____

6a. Which is more effective: information from autobiographical sources, or information from experts?
  b. Is there any danger in autobiographical information?
7. Should you be a "ratfink" on others who are smoking pot?

=====================================

> If your child is a recurrent heavy drug user — and I mean chemicals — it's too late. You've blown your cool a long time ago. You've had it as a parent.
>
> Dr. L. Solursh
> psychiatrist

=====================================

Drugs and the Law

Since punitive laws, deterent sentences, and zealous police enforcement have failed not only to eradicate the use of marijuana but have even failed to prevent its widespread proliferation, we must examine the *practice* of the law, as well as the theory to determine what effect the law has had in regulating the conditions of sale of marijuana.

The first point is that of *quality control*. As the drug is illegal there is no way that the buyer can be protected by inspection of the content of the marijuana sold. When we buy a bottle of liquor we know exactly what we are getting because the dosage of ethyl alcohol is clearly labelled on the outside. The pot smoker buys an unknown commodity. He may be paying for oregano or green tea or crushed basil leaves or even catnip. He may be getting a large proportion of material from the inactive male plant. All this will be quite harmless, although a waste of money. But there are reports of toxic impurities being found in marijuana, and reports of bad reactions on the part of smokers who are quite capable of handling marijuana, as such. There are also reports of distributors mixing heroin with marijuana in order to hook young people on hard narcotics.[1] Some regular users express great concern about this. Actually, this fear may be very exaggerated. It is doubtful, medically, that persons can become addicted to heroin unknowingly or unwittingly. . . .

This also brings up another point. In order to produce and distribute an illegal commodity an illegal sales network is necessary, as well as a subculture of drug users. In such an environment both profit motives and social encourage multiple drug use. Pot smokers may take LSD, or take amphetamines and become speed freaks. It is my impression that most of the traffic in marijuana is still in the hands of young people. But even here there is a strong incentive to try other, more dangerous, hallucinogenics and amphetamine drugs. The more the laws are enforced, the more the traffic is harassed, the higher the prices become and the more incentive there is for organized criminal elements to move in on the market — and the more likely it is that heroin will be made available. A moralistic law thus turns out in practice to have a quite different effect than that intended by its framers.

---

[1]"Pushers add heroin to marijuana to attract new addicts, MP says," *Globe and Mail* (Nov. 1, 1967).

A particularly distasteful aspect of the marijuana law situation is the use of police undercover agents to infiltrate groups of young marijuana users and to entrap them into selling some drugs. There is something very unedifying about an agent posing as a youth's friend or associate and instigating a criminal offence for which the unfortunate youth may pay dearly. There are very real questions of public morality involved in this matter, particularly when some testimony has indicated that on occasion the agent has persistently sought to make a purchase from an unwilling source. Should an action undertaken to oblige a friend be placed on the same legal footing as a carefully planned criminal operation undertaken for personal gain? An exceptionally revolting use of undercover agents occurred at Cornell University in New York State, where an agent posing as a student actually conducted an affair with a girl who, upon complying with her boyfriend's request for some pot, was promptly arrested. She was eventually acquitted, but on a legal technicality, not on the gross immorality of the police behavior. Not surprisingly there is a good deal of paranoia afoot among youth about the activities of the "narcs". When even high school students begin seeing police spies behind every telephone pole we have gone a long way down the road to a police state. And what is the net effect of all these activities? After a few months of undercover activity there is a grand bust and a number of bedraggled hippies are thrown into jail. The newspapers are full of headlines that proclaim DOPE RING SMASHED or NARCOTICS RAID NETS HIPPIE DRUG PEDDLERS. Out in the suburbs, Mr. and Mrs. Middle-Class Canada go to bed feeling safer that night. And meanwhile the number of pot smokers continues to increase as if nothing had happened.

A new twist to the scene has been added by attempts to encourage parents to turn their children in to the police if they find drugs in their possession. According to a newspaper report, "In Seattle, the police encourage parents to provide information that would be useful in prosecuting their children and even to testify against them in court. Many parents co-operate 'because they feel what's right is right', a police spokesman said." In Ottawa recently a teen-age girl was turned in by her parents when a small amount of hashish was found in her room. The magistrate commended them for their "concern" for their "daughter's welfare," and their "faith in our legal system". Parents ought to be aware that they are doing their children far more lasting harm by offering them up on the bloody altar of an insane law. Children who become involved in drugs may well need help, but help is the last thing that the law, in its present state, can offer. You do not cure your child's infected finger by chopping off his hand.

8. Would legalizing pot make its use more widespread or less popular? Would legalizing it make more people turn to harder drugs, or keep people from using them?
9. What would be the results if the use of marijuana was not legalized, but simply ignored by the law?
10. What proposals would you make regarding marijuana laws?
11. Are parents doing the right thing if they "turn in" their children for using marijuana?

=====

No, they shouldn't legalize marijuana. Even if it's not addictive, it's still an escape. Anybody using it is still trying to escape.

heroin addict,
aged 17.

=====

Drugs As Part Of A Culture

One of the methods used by societies to manage the drug experience is to allow one or two drugs to assume an accepted place in social organization, elaborately bound about with ritual, religious significance, and strictly prescribed usage, and at the same time to violently oppose the use of any other unapproved drug. In this way, certain drugs have become assimilated into a culture, and thus pacified. The important point is that this process has very little to do with the pharmacology of the drug, but a great deal to do with the needs of the culture. Almost all known drugs, even those considered most dangerous to us, have an accepted place in some culture or other. And the reverse is also true. Hashish (or marijuana) has been accommodated in Middle Eastern Islamic society, while alcohol is a dreaded menace specifically proscribed by the Koran. Here in the West, of course, the exact opposite holds. Certain coca leaves were sacred to the ancient Incas, but cocaine, a derivative of coca, was once a dangerous drug among North American criminals. Indians of Western North America have elaborated an entire religious experience around the use of peyote, an LSD-like drug which we apparently feel to be extremely menacing, and yet the Indians are notoriously unable to handle alcohol.

In fact, the introduction of a new drug into a culture unprepared to cope with it can have a devastating effect. The settlers who took Canada from the Indians were well aware of this. The whisky bottle was a prime weapon in the campaign of cultural disorganization waged by the white invaders. On the other hand, cultural paranoia about strange drugs can also take on bizarre dimensions. Such an utterly innocuous substance as chocolate, for instance, roused a storm of violent disapproval when it was first introduced into Europe following its discovery in Mexico, on the absurd grounds that it was an aphrodisiac, and would lead its users, especially women, into a life of licence and debauchery.[1]

When coffee was first discovered in the Middle East, the official reaction was much the same as our present reaction to marijuana. In sixteenth century Egypt, sales were banned, stocks burned, persons were convicted of having drunk the evil substance, and warnings denouncing its pernicious properties were circulated widely. Eventually its use became so widespread that all the laws against it were repealed and coffee became a normal part of Middle Eastern life.[2] The use of tobacco in North America demonstrates even more vividly the cyclical nature of social response to drugs. In the nineteenth century, a long struggle was waged against cigarettes, which led the *New York Times* to solemnly warn its readers in 1884 that "the decadence of Spain began when the Spaniards adopted cigarettes and if this pernicious practice obtains among adult Americans the ruin of the Republic is close at hand."[3] Gradually cigarette smoking has become so popular that strong social pressures are exerted to encourage people to smoke. Now that the connection between cigarettes and lung cancer has become apparent, the government is faced with the gargantuan task of trying to change the social mores so as to make smoking once again unpopular.

In a sense, certain drugs may take on symbolic meanings, as representing different styles of life. Alcohol in our society has delicate nuances of class designation attached to the various forms in which it is consumed: the beer-drinking worker in the pub is socially distant from the wine-tasting gourmet in the restaurant, and each is apt to have a low opinion of the other's

---

[1]Norman Taylor, *Narcotics: Nature's Dangerous Gifts* (New York, Dell, 1963), pp. 181-89.

[2]Robert S. DeRopp, *Drugs and the Mind* (New York, Grove Press, 1957), p. 248.

[3]Taylor, *op. cit.,* p. 104.

tastes. Although both tea and coffee contain caffeine, tea is extremely popular in Britain, while coffee is virtually unchallenged in the United States (Canada, as always, rests somewhere between these two poles). Somehow the coffee break has become a characteristic of the North American work day, while 3 o'clock tea has remained specifically British. Cigars are associated with aggressive businessmen, and pipes, which were once considered a lower-class symbol, are now associated with the affluent college-educated elite.

Such symbolism, mild and imprecise enough when the drugs concerned are more or less approved, becomes much more formidable when the drug is banned by the society. To the average North American, alcohol is the mark of the outgoing, aggressive, success-oriented personality so prized by business organizations. Conversely, the opium-smoking Oriental might seem to be a shiftless, lazy, good-for-nothing degenerate. To the Oriental, however, the smoking of opium might appear to impart a certain philosophical tranquillity, a passive dignity more in keeping with the traditional virtues than the crude, belligerent drunkenness of the North American.

The cultural relativism of any statements about drugs should now be clear. One would have to be either very ethnocentric or very foolhardy to make resoundingly absolute statements about any drugs based solely on one cultural perspective (and if we are honest with ourselves, one class or status position within that culture). Nor is it good enough to try to wriggle out of this dilemma by saying that whatever *our* culture says must at any rate be accepted for *us,* since the whole wrangle about drugs today turns precisely on the question of *what* our culture actually does say, and, perhaps more importantly who speaks for 'our culture' in the first place.

12. How does this passage attempt to explain why our society is so upset about drug use?

13a. What is the author's purpose in comparing the introduction of drugs into our culture with the introduction of such items as coffee, chocolate, and alcohol into other cultures?
  b. Is this a logical comparison?
14. Who is best equipped to speak about the place of drugs in our culture:

> drug users?
> non-drugs users?
> doctors?
> social scientists?
> policemen?

15. Why has our society reacted with such fear toward drugs?

THINK

(a) Resolved: That drugs are for weaklings.
(b) Alcohol is acknowledged to be a factor in some crimes, accidents, and social disorders. If government made alcohol illegal, would young people be more disposed toward restrictive laws on drugs?
(c) "Because drugs are an inward-turning device, their use indicates outward decay. There is no question that the current popularity of drug use indicates an imminent collapse of our civilization." Is this a logical statement?
(d) What are some of the reasons which explain why this particular generation of young people has developed what some call a "drug subculture"?
(e) Thrilling and potentially dangerous sports like parachute-jumping or speedboat racing cause participants and spectators to produce a lot of adrenalin. Is this, in essence, any different from taking drugs to experience a "high" feeling?
(f) Our society is a great user of "above-ground" drugs. To what extent does this affect the popularity of marijuana and other drugs?
(g) From the class collect all the supposed "facts" both for and against marijuana, LSD, amphetamines, heroin, and opium. How many of the "facts" have been *conclusively proven* by scientific evidence?

5. THEY CALL IT SPORT

Football, 1583

from The Anatomie Of Abuses,
written in 1583 by Philip Stubbes

For as concerning football playing, I protest unto you it may rather be called a friendly kind of fight, than a play or recreation; a bloody and murdering practice, than a fellowly sport or pastime. For doth not every one lie in wait for his adversary, seeking to overthrow him and pick him on the nose, though it be upon hard stones, in ditch or dale, or what place soever it be he careth not, so he have him down. And he that can serve the most of this fashion, he is counted the only fellow, and who but he? So that by this means, sometimes their necks are broken, sometimes their backs, sometimes their legs, sometimes their arms, sometimes one part thrust out of joint, sometimes another, sometimes their noses gush out with blood, sometimes their eyes start out, and sometimes hurt in one place, sometimes in another. But whosoever scapeth away the best goeth not scot free, but is either sore wounded and bruised, so as he dieth of it, or else scapeth very hardly. And no marvel, for they have sleights to meet one betwixt two, to dash him against the heart with the elbows, to hit him under the short ribs with their gripped fists, and with their knees to catch him upon the hip, and to pick him on the neck, with an hundred such murdering devices. And hereof groweth envy, rancour, choler, hatred, displeasure, enmity and what not else; and sometimes fighting, brawling, contention, quarrel-picking, murder, homicide and great effusion of blood, as experience daily teacheth.

1. Can a sport justifiably be called *cruel* when those who take part in it do so of their own free will?
2. Do Stubbes' objections seem to be based on a moral or a humanitarian point-of-view?
3. With Stubbes' idiom, and his outlook, describe any modern contact sport. (Compare your results with any example of modern sport idiom.)

Sports In A Sociological Context

Since our society is founded on myths, half-truths, and vague understandings of natural process, it is only normal that we would also operate under the misapprehension that sports are a test of physical stamina and dexterity, and of cooperative spirit.

The truth is that most sport is based on animal cunning, animal strength, and emotional blood-lust. Boxing is a prime example. A report by England's Royal College of Physicians revealed that of 229 professional boxers active between 1929 and 1955, one out of six had serious brain damage, and one out of three was walking around "punchdrunk." The U.S. National Research Council recently discovered that in professional football in America, injuries requiring major surgery or six weeks in a cast, occur once every 357 times the ball is put into play. (36 football players died of injuries in the U.S. during 1968). Comparable statistics in auto racing, professional hockey and other sports are equally shocking. Yet, by most sportsmen, these deaths and injuries are considered to be "part of the game."

Such inhumanity is intolerable in a society which spends millions in research to prevent death and injury, a society which literally would move a mountain to save a single life.

Objective analysis of the current state of sports leads to some clear-cut conclusions. In the first place the situation is becoming worse. Relatively harmless sports like baseball, cricket or tennis are declining in spectator value whereas injury-prone games like football, hockey, and now roller-derby, show greatly increased attendance rates. The fact is that our society, inured as it is to violence, is coming to demand such bloodletting activities as a means of sublimation.

A second conclusion only becoming apparent as this century passes, is that the popularity of cruel sports is generally indicative of a decline in civilization. Gladiatorial combat in Rome reached its greatest height of popularity after the Empire had passed its zenith. The same holds true of the popularity of jousting tournaments in the feudal era. Now in the twentieth century, our own decadence is reflected in our so-called sporting activities.

The third and perhaps most subtle factor is the "stable-ethos." Blood and economics have now joined forces. Players are *owned* by the team for which they play. This is a necessity in view of the huge amounts of money needed to maintain and promote a team. An *owner* has, in effect, his own stable of players who can be bought, sold, and traded like so many cattle. And like cattle they are fed, trained, and equipped to be made suitable for public slaughter.

The time has come for the myth to be exploded. It is no accident that an old and little-used meaning of the word "sport" is:

one who is strikingly deviate from the normal.

4. ". . . our society is founded on myths, half-truths, and vague understandings of natural process. . . ." To what extent is this true? Is the *true meaning* of sport a myth?
5. Present arguments that counter the three conclusions the writer has made.
6. Is there more, or less skill in contact sports like hockey and football, as opposed to sports like tennis or track and field?

<hr>

The boy's a beautiful brute, he loves to hang 'em on the glass.

New York Daily News reporter,
describing a hockey player

To Hunt Or Not To Hunt

from They Call It Sport

by James McAree

Implicit in any conception of sport is the principle that the protagonists should be more or less equally matched. When a hunter sets out to track down a grizzly bear he takes his life in his hands. He knows that if the circumstances are favourable, the bear will kill him. It is so with the hunting of all large and ferocious animals. The hunter has his gun, the prey has its claws, its teeth and its cunning, and it has the added advantage that the deadly game is being played on its home grounds. The deer, on the other hand, has only its speed and the fact that nature gives it a coat that helps camouflage it from the hunter's eyes. Even this last advantage is lost when the dogs start it running, for it is bound to pass close to some spot where a hunter is ready and waiting for it.

So far as the hunter is concerned, the element of risk is wholly absent. He is never in the slightest danger. A hundred deer could provide no menace. He is really an executioner, not a duellist.

And the deer has done him no harm. Now and then it is true that deer will invade cultivated fields and do some damage; or, when they are starving and have been driven by wolves, they will help themselves from a haystack in a farmyard. On such occasions, a case could possibly be made out for killing them. But here again it can hardly be regarded as a sport. It is an unpleasant duty, a phase of self-protection.

In recent years there has grown up a sentiment against the wanton killing of wild animals which in some circumstances may be dangerous. But the truth is that in the great majority of cases the wildest of animals do not trouble man until troubled by man. Quite different is the killing of wild beasts when they themselves have learned to prey on human beings, like the old and almost toothless tiger which is no longer capable of killing his natural prey and has found that human beings are easy to kill and perhaps pleasant to eat. Hunters go into the woods and track down these menaces and are applauded and rewarded when they succeed and that is quite right. There is, too, some justification for the general sentiment which approves killing as a sport when the animal killed is itself a killer, living on other creatures which have an equal right to exist.

Yes, there sometimes are reasons to kill an animal. Sometimes. But in Canada the occasions are few. Yet you'll find the callous hunter well stocked with arguments to justify, in his own mind at least, his gory "sport". Take the old chestnut about wolves, for instance. The hunter argues this way: if he does not kill the deer, the wolves will, and if the deer are permitted to multiply so will the wolves. In the end, he insists, we may have to fight for our very lives against them.

What nonsense! Obviously the way to meet such a danger, if such a danger is possible, is to kill the wolves—not the deer. If the hunter is sincere in his wish to render the country a service, the method is clear enough. In fact, if the hunter is really interested in "sport" the idea of hunting down a beast of prey should have much more appeal than the slaughter of innocent animals. To hunt down a wolf or wolf pack would be a much more ticklish business than to cut down a defenceless deer, for a wolf, an ugly customer if cornered, has at least some way of fighting for his life. In ridding the country of a menacing beast of prey, a hunter might feel that he was discharging a social duty. Can any hunter feel the same way about slaughtering a deer?

There are proper ways of regulating the deer population, if ever that should become necessary, without leaving it to the sportsmen or the wolves. It is the general feeling of game wardens and others whose business it is to see that nobody kills more than his legal limit that as many deer are killed illegally as legally. It is impossible that we should have a game warden for every man in the woods with a rifle. The killing can only be checked when the hunters come out of the woods and are on their way home.

This whole business of killing harmless, innocent animals in the name of sport is a vicious thing. How can anyone with humane instincts lift a gun to his shoulder and reduce a fine, handsome creature to a bloody mess?

7. Is hunting more cruel than sports like boxing or bull-fighting?
8. "There is, too, some justification for the general sentiment which approves killing as a sport when the animal killed is itself a killer, . . ."
   McAree published this essay in 1950. Is that argument viable today?
9. Why are governments reluctant to curb hunting practices?

$port$

Shooting an eagle three on the seventeenth hole in the Master's; breaking a ninth inning tie in the World Series with a home run in the left field stands; picking off a forty yard pass in the end zone in the last quarter of the Grey Cup— these are the moments that live forever in the heart of a player. They also live in his bank account. Every time a professional athlete does something significant in his particular game, he increases his endorsement potential and sells stock in his enterprises.

Whether or not it is an evil, it is certainly a fact that most of the prominent figures in sports today earn a large percentage of their income, not from their sports activity but from the commercial value that grows from it. Arnold Palmer golf equipment—Mickey Mantle restaurants—Jean Beliveau Inc. —even the Olympics, the symbol of purity in sport, has contributed Bob Richards to the sale of Wheaties.

The idea is definitely to the financial advantage of the players. Aside from the income their ventures attract, there are tax advantages, and because the enterprises need a manager, they are usually free of all the problems of handling money.

But for active players at least, there are some drawbacks. Big business takes time, and this means time away from drills, practice, and planning sessions. Other players resent the advantages enjoyed by the stars, and fans tend to look askance at sub-par performances by their executive-heroes.

Then there are ethical and moral issues which are still undebated. There is the question, for example, of whether a professional athlete, because of his large and headlong following of young children, is, in fact, using immoral propaganda techniques in urging the purchase of his products.

More than anything, however, what lies in precarious balance because of these commercial inroads, is the very future of sport itself. The value of sport has always been inherent in the teamwork and skill of the players, and the vicarious pleasure of spectators who share in the performance. What may happen to these important features is yet unknown.

*   *   *

10. Is it immoral for a sports figure with a large following of children to endorse a particular product?
11a. What are the dangers to the future of sport if this commercialism continues?
  b. Is there a danger to society at large, if this practice were to be stopped by legislation?

A leading sports columnist in a large Canadian city once said that his pick for athlete of the year would be a professional wrestler, for wrestlers admit that everything about their sport is phony, and act accordingly.

All In The Cause Of Good Fellowship

from Shooting An Elephant
by George Orwell

I am always amazed when I hear people saying that sport creates goodwill between nations, and that if only the common peoples of the world could meet one another at football or cricket, they would have no inclination to meet on the battle-field. Even if one didn't know from concrete examples (the 1936 Olympic Games, for instance) that international sporting contests lead to orgies of hatred, one could deduce it from general principles.

Nearly all the sports practised nowadays are competitive. You play to win, and the game has little meaning unless you do your utmost to win. On the village green, where you pick up sides and no feeling of local patriotism is involved, it is possible to play simply for the fun and exercise: but as soon as the question of prestige arises, as soon as you feel that you and some larger unit will be disgraced if you lose, the most savage combative instincts are aroused. Anyone who has played even in a school football match knows this. At the international level sport is frankly mimic warfare. But the significant thing is not the behaviour of the players but the attitude of the spectators: and, behind the spectators, of the nations who work themselves into furies over these absurd contests, and seriously believe—at any rate for short periods— that running, jumping and kicking a ball are tests of national virtue.

In England, the obsession with sport is bad enough, but even fiercer passions are aroused in young countries where game-playing and nationalism are both recent developments. In countries like India or Burma, it is necessary at football matches to have strong cordons of people to keep the crowd from invading the field. In Burma, I have seen the supporters of one side break through the police and disable the goalkeeper of the opposing side at a critical moment. The first big football match that was played in Spain about fifteen years ago led to an uncontrollable riot. As soon as strong feelings of rivalry are aroused, the notion of playing the game according to the rules always vanishes. People want to see one side on top and the other side humiliated and they forget that victory gained through cheating or through the intervention of the crowd is meaningless. Even when the spectators don't intervene physically they try to influence the game by cheering their own side and "rattling" opposing players with boos and insults. Serious sport has nothing to do with fair play. It is bound up with hatred, jealousy, boastfulness, disregard of all rules and sadistic pleasure in witnessing violence: in other words it is war minus the shooting.

Instead of blah-blahing about the clean, healthy rivalry of the football field and the great part played by the Olympic Games in bringing the nations together, it is more useful to inquire how and why this modern cult of sport arose. Most of the games we now play are of ancient origin, but sport does not seem to have been taken very seriously between Roman times and the nineteenth century. Even in the English public schools the games cult did not start till the later part of the last century. Dr. Arnold, generally regarded as the founder of the modern public school, looked on games as simply a waste of time. Then, chiefly in England and the United States, games were built up into a heavily financed activity, capable of attracting vast crowds and rousing savage passions, and the infection spread from country to country. It is the most violently combative sports, football and boxing, that have spread the widest. There cannot be much doubt that the whole thing is bound up with the rise of nationalism—that is, with the lunatic habit of identifying oneself with large power units and seeing everything in terms of competitive prestige. Also, organized games are more likely to flourish in urban communities where the average human being lives a sedentary or at least a confined life, and does not get much opportunity for creative labour. In a rustic community a boy or young man works off a good deal of his surplus energy by walking, swimming, snowballing, climbing trees, riding horses, and by various sports involving cruelty to animals, such as fishing, cockfighting and ferreting for rats. In a big town one must indulge in group activities if one wants an outlet for one's physical strength or for one's sadistic impulses. Games are taken seriously in London and New York, and they were taken seriously in Rome and Byzantium: in the Middle Ages they were played, and probably played with much physical brutality, but they were not mixed up with politics nor a cause of group hatreds.

When the National Hockey League doubled the number of teams in the 1960's, franchises sold for *millions* of dollars. When a member of one of the new teams died as a result of head injuries, the league set aside *$5000* for research to develop an effective helmet.

If you wanted to add to the vast fund of ill-will existing in the world at this moment, you could hardly do it better than by a series of football matches between Jews and Arabs, Germans and Czechs, Indians and British, Russians and Poles, and Italians and Yugoslavs, each match to be watched by a mixed audience of 100,000 spectators. I do not, of course, suggest that sport is one of the main causes of international rivalry; big-scale sport is itself, I think, merely another effect of the causes that have produced nationalism. Still, you do make things worse by sending forth a team of eleven men, labelled as national champions, to do battle against some rival team, and allowing it to be felt on all sides that whichever nation is defeated will "lose face".

*　　　　*　　　　*

12. What is Orwell's basic criticism of organized sport?
13. Is the philosophy expressed in this article consistent with the way of thinking expressed in Orwell's novels, *1984* and *Animal Farm?*
13. Are Orwell's views extreme?
14. Why did he mention the 1936 Olympics? To what extent does the spirit of the 1936 Olympics prevail today?
15. Why does the popularity of organized sport seem to be contingent upon civilized conditions such as ours?

THINK

(a) Write an apologia:
   (i) for sport generally
   (ii) for organized sport
   (iii) for professional sport
(b) Produce a brief but comprehensive definition of sport.
(c) Resolved: That athletics are a means of proving masculinity otherwise unavailable to certain men for reasons such as lack of intelligence.
(d) Does a sport which is popular in a particular geographical area indicate to any degree the prevailing characteristic of the people of the area? (In your analysis, be sure to include some of the more esoteric sporting activities such as throwing-the-hammer, cock-fighting, and fighting-fish.)
(e) To what extent is sport an integral part of our society?
(f) Develop a presentation which explains sports activity as a natural outgrowth of the human psyche.

6. PROTEST— DISSENT? OR VIOLENCE?

KILL THE PIG

URN BABY, BURN

LIBERTY!
EQUALITY!
FRATERNITY!

BLACK

VIVE LE QUEBEC LIBRE

Hell no! we wo

> Perseverance is more prevailing than violence; and
> many things which cannot be overcome when they
> are together, yield themselves up when taken little
> by little.
>
> Quintus Sertorius,
> Roman General, 72, B.C.

Why They Won't Fight

by William Spenser

David Millen is a shy, fair-haired 18-year-old from Detroit,
Michigan. He had arrived in Montreal two days before with
a friend, and the ADC* had moved them into a basement flat.

Lacking two credits towards his high school diploma, Dave
had enlisted in the US army on May 27, 1969. Dave thought
he would become "independent" in the army, but soon discovered he was just a number.

Sent to Fort Knox, Kentucky, for eight weeks' basic training, Dave had trouble fitting in almost immediately. "I had
emotional difficulties," he said, "and I couldn't conform to the
discipline. At home, I had been taught to think like a man,
but here you were just like cattle. There was no room for
individuality."

Sent to another company to continue his training, Dave
went AWOL for 12 days in Detroit, where he did a lot of
thinking, but didn't go home. He decided to go back, received
a summary court martial, a demotion to private E-1, the lowest

---

*ADC—a group in Montreal that helps army deserters and others
who wish to avoid the draft.

rank, and a fine of two-thirds of a month's pay ($76). Still, he graduated from basic training and was transferred to Fort Sam Houston, Texas, for advanced training. Dave spent 13 weeks preparing to be a medic, and at the end of it, received orders for Vietnam.

Home on leave, Dave decided to desert. He obtained the address of the ADC and was driven to Windsor, where he and his friend caught a train for Montreal.

A guitarist who played with a group called The Third World War in Detroit, Dave would like to study piano, and work for a degree in music. But for the moment, he is trying to adjust to his new surroundings.

"I feel I am coming to the age of manhood," he explained. "I don't feel I am a man yet, although the army gave me a foothold on this. But I have to do what I truly feel is right."

———————————————

... unless there is a method, be it through elections or otherwise, by which the governed can make their views effective in some proportion to their weight, the nation is at the mercy of violence in the form of terrorism, assassination, conspiracy, mass compulsion, and civil war.

In Defence of Liberalism, 1934

———————————————

Front de libération du Québec

1963   sixty-five year old watchman killed by bomb in Montreal.

dynamite placed in fifteen mail boxes. Five explode.

Explosives expert crippled for life.

1964   holdup and thefts of weapons and munitions.

unsuccessful holdup of International Firearms store in Montreal. Two killed.

publicity develops regarding commando style training centre in Northern Quebec.

1965   fairly quiet year. Two trains derailed.

1966   office employee killed by bomb.

1968   twenty-one bombings or attempted bombings including Montreal city hall.

1969   Montreal stock exchange bombed; twenty-seven injured.

home of Montreal mayor bombed.

developing publicity regarding training of FLQ in guerrilla warfare by Arab guerrillas in Middle East.

1970   explosive kills Ottawa civil servant.

1970   *The October Crisis*

In October 1970, the FLQ terrified the entire Canadian nation by kidnapping a British diplomat, James Cross, and also shortly after, the Quebec Minister of Labor, Pierre LaPorte. Shortly before the terror was escalated even further by the murder of Pierre LaPorte, the Canadian government took an unprecedented step in peacetime, by invoking the War Measures Act. The following passage contains excerpts from a speech to the Canadian nation by Prime Minister Trudeau explaining the reasons for such a drastic decision.

Protest — Dissent? Or Violence?   89

NOTES FROM A NATIONAL BROADCAST BY THE
PRIME MINISTER OF CANADA

The governments of Canada and Quebec have been told by groups of self-styled revolutionaries that they intend to murder in cold blood two innocent men unless their demands are met. The kidnappers claim they act as they do in order to draw attention to instances of social injustice. But I ask them whose attention are they seeking to attract. The Government of Canada? The Government of Quebec? Every government in this country is well aware of the existence of deep and important social problems. And every government to the limit of its resources and ability is deeply committed to their solution. But not by kidnappings and bombings. By hard work. And if any doubt exists about the good faith or the ability of any government, there are opposition parties ready and willing to be given an opportunity to govern. In short there is available everywhere in Canada an effective mechanism to change governments by peaceful means. It has been employed by disenchanted voters again and again.

*   *   *

What are the kidnappers demanding in return for the lives of these men? Several things. For one, they want their grievances aired by force in public on the assumption, no doubt, that all right-thinking persons would be persuaded that the problems of the world can be solved by shouting slogans and insults.

They want more, they want the police to offer up as a sacrificial lamb a person whom they assume assisted in the lawful arrest and proper conviction of certain of their criminal friends. They also want money. Ransom money.

They want still more. They demand the release from prison of 17 criminals, and the dropping of charges against 6 other men, all of whom they refer to as "political prisoners". Who are these men who are held out as latter-day patriots and martyrs? Let me describe them to you.

Three are convicted murderers; five others were jailed for manslaughter; one is serving a life imprisonment after having pleaded guilty to numerous charges related to bombings; another has been convicted of 17 armed robberies; two were once parolled but are now back in jail awaiting trial on charges of robberies.

Yet we are being asked to believe that these persons have been unjustly dealt with, that they have been imprisoned as a result of their political opinions, and that they deserve to be freed immediately, without recourse to due process of law.

*　　*　　*

Let me turn now to the broader implications of the threat represented by the FLQ and similar organizations.

If a democratic society is to continue to exist, it must be able to root out the cancer of an armed, revolutionary movement that is bent on destroying the very basis of our freedom. For that reason the Government, following an analysis of the facts, including requests of the Government of Quebec and the City of Montreal for urgent action, decided to proclaim the War Measures Act. It did so at 4:00 a.m. this morning, in order to permit the full weight of Government to be brought quickly to bear on all those persons advocating or practising violence as a means of achieving political ends.

The War Measures Act gives sweeping powers to the Government. It also suspends the operation of the Canadian Bill of Rights. I can assure you that the Government is most reluctant to seek such powers, and did so only when it became crystal clear that the situation could not be controlled unless some extraordinary assistance was made available on an urgent basis.

The authority contained in the Act will permit Governments to deal effectively with the nebulous yet dangerous challenge to society represented by the terrorist organizations. The criminal law as it stands is simply not adequate to deal with systematic terrorism.

The police have therefore been given certain extraordinary powers necessary for the effective detection and elimination of conspiratorial organizations which advocate the use of violence. These organizations, and membership in them, have been declared illegal. The powers include the right to search and arrest without warrant, to detain suspected persons without the necessity of laying specific charges immediately, and to detain persons without bail.

* * *

I recognize, as I hope do others, that this extreme position into which governments have been forced is in some respects a trap. It is a well-known technique of revolutionary groups who attempt to destroy society by unjustified violence to goad the authorities into inflexible attitudes. The revolutionaries then employ this evidence of alleged authoritarianism as justification for the need to use violence in their renewed attacks on the social structure. I appeal to all Canadians not to become so obsessed by what the government has done today in response to terrorism that they forget the opening play in this vicious game. That play was taken by the revolutionaries; they chose to use bombing, murder and kidnapping.

* * *

This government is not acting out of fear. It is acting to prevent fear from spreading. It is acting to maintain the rule of law without which freedom is impossible. It is acting to make clear to kidnappers and revolutionaries and assassins that in this country laws are made and changed by the elected representatives of all Canadians—not by a handful of self-selected dictators—those who gain power through terror, rule through terror. The government is acting, therefore, to protect your life and your liberty.

* * *

There are very few times in the history of any country when all persons must take a stand on critical issues. This is one of those times; this is one of those issues. I am confident that those persons who unleashed this tragic sequence of events with the aim of destroying our society and dividing our country will find that the opposite will occur. The result of their acts will be a stronger society in a unified country. Those who would have divided us will have united us.

Rt. Hon. Pierre E. Trudeau

1. Is a democracy being undemocratic when it takes away the rights of citizens in order to protect them?
2. Many people feel, consciously or subconsciously, that democracy is an act of faith.
   a. Is this true for you?
   b. Do you agree that the Prime Minister in his speech was appealing to this attitude?
3. Most Canadians—even those who oppose the Prime Minister —gave great praise to this speech. Analyze the excerpts carefully, and consider why the speech received such overwhelming support.
4a. Most revolutions are started and won by a minority. Why?
   b. How does Mr. Trudeau explain, and respond to this fact?
   c. By means of some research, try to find out how many successful revolutions in the past, failed miserably in their first attempts.
5. Obtain a copy of the War Measures Act by writing a member of Parliament, or by writing the House of Commons, Ottawa. What are the implications for you if this act should ever be invoked again?

I discovered in the earliest stages that pursuit of truth did not permit violence being inflicted on one's opponent, but that he must be weaned from error by patience and sympathy.

Mahatma Ghandi, 1939

Conscience For Change

by Martin Luther King

The generation of the past 25 years cannot be understood without remembering that it has lived during that period through the effects of four wars: World War II, the "cold war," the Korean War, and Vietnam. No other generation of young Americans was ever exposed to a remotely similar traumatic experience. Yet as spiritually and physically abrasive as this may be, it is not the worst aspect of contemporary experience. This is the first generation to grow up in the era of the nuclear bomb, knowing that it may be the last generation of mankind.

This is the generation not only of war, but of war in its ultimate revelation. This is the generation that truly has no place to hide, and no place to find security.

There are evils enough to send reason reeling. And of course they are not the only ones. All of them form part of the matrix in which this generation's character and experience were formed. The tempest of evils provides the answer for those adults who ask why this young generation is so unfathomable, so alienated, and frequently so freakish. For the young people of today, peace and social tranquility are as unreal and remote as knight errantry.

Under the impact of social forces unique to their times, young people have splintered into three principal groups, though of course there is some overlap among the three.

The largest group of young people is struggling to adapt itself to the prevailing values of our society. Without much enthusiasm, they accept the system of government, the economic relationship of the property system, and the social stratifications both engender. But even so, they are a profoundly troubled group, and are harsh critics of the *status quo*.

In this largest group, social attitudes are not congealed or determined; they are fluid and searching. Though all recent studies point to the fact that the war in Vietnam is a focus of concern, most of them are not ready to resist the Draft or to take clear-cut stands on issues of violence and non-violence. But their consciences have been touched by the feeling that is growing, all over the world, of the horror and insanity of war, of the imperative need to respect life, of the urgency of moving past war as a way to solve international problems. So while they will not glorify war, and while they feel ambiguous about America's military posture, this majority group reflects the confusion of the larger society, which is itself caught up in a kind of transitional state of conscience as it moves slowly toward the realization that war can not be justified in the human future.

There is a second group of young people, the radicals. They range from moderate to extreme in the degree to which they want to alter the social system. All of them agree that only by *structural* change can current evils be eliminated, because the roots are in the system rather than in men or in faulty operation. These are a new breed of radicals. Very few adhere to any established ideology; some borrow from old doctrines of revolution; but practically all of them suspend judgment on what the form of a new society must be. They are in serious revolt against old values and have not yet concretely formulated the new ones. They are not repeating previous revolutionary doctrines; most of them have not even read the revolutionary classics. Ironically, their rebelliousness comes from having been frustrated in seeking change within the framework of the existing society. They tried to build racial equality, and met tenacious and vicious opposition. They worked to end the Vietnam War, and experienced futility. So they seek a fresh start with new rules in a new order. It is fair to say, though, that at present they know what they don't want rather than what they do want. Their radicalism is growing because the power structure of today is unrelenting in defending not only its social system, but the evils it contains; so, naturally, it is intensifying the opposition.

What is the attitude of this second radical group to the problem of violence? In a word, mixed; there are young radicals to-day who are pacifists, and there are others who are armchair revolutionaries who insist on the political and psychological need for violence. These young theorists of violence elaborately scorn the process of dialogue in favor of the "tactics of confrontation"; they glorify the guerrilla movement and especially its new martyr, Che Guevara; and they equate revolutionary consciousness with the readiness to shed blood. But across the spectrum of attitudes towards violence that can be found among the radicals is there a unifying thread? I think there is. Whether they read Ghandi or Franz Fannon, all the radicals understand the need for action—direct self-transforming and structure-transforming action. This may be their most creative, collective insight.

The young people in the third group are currently called "hippies". They may be traced in a fairly direct line from yesterday's beatniks. The hippies are not only colorful, but complex; and in many respects their extreme conduct illuminates the negative effect of society's evils on sensitive young people. While there are variations, those who identify with this group have a common philosophy.

They are struggling to disengage from society as their expression of their rejection of it. They disavow responsibility to organized society. Unlike the radicals, they are not seeking change, but flight. When occasionally they merge with a peace demonstration, it is not to better the political world, but to give expression to their own world. The hard-core hippy is a remarkable contradiction. He uses drugs to turn inward, away from reality, to find peace and security. Yet he advocates love as the highest human value—love, which can exist only in communication between people, and not in the total isolation of the individual.

The importance of the hippies is not in their unconventional behavior, but in the fact that some hundreds of thousands of young people, in turning to a flight from reality, are expressing a profoundly discrediting judgment on the society they emerge from.

6. How does each of the groups described here, view contemporary society? Specifically, how is each group reacting to its feelings?
7. In King's opinion, what are the root causes of unrest in the young generation? Are there any other basic causes which you feel he should have included?
8. Does his division into three groups adequately describe the fabric of protest today?
9. Does Martin Luther King take the side of any one of the groups?
10a. What benefit does he suggest will come from all the protest?
  b. Which group do you feel will ultimately be most effective in bringing about change?

SURVIVAL KIT

from RAT Magazine, *New York*

So far the pigs have used five kinds of gas on people—two kinds of tear gas, nausea gas, blister gas, and mace. There are ways to deal with most of them.

Wear heavy clothing so your skin isn't exposed to blister powder or nausea gas, both of which affect your skin. If you're really badly burned or gassed, get to a medical center. Don't rub your eyes at all when you've been gassed.

Last year people thought vaseline was the answer to gas. It's not. It makes mace worse if you can't wipe it off instantly.

And it always makes tear gas worse. So you shouldn't use it.

A good gas mask is protection against mace and tear gas. But most gas masks people have are cheap and no good. They leak or trap gas near your face. Also if you're wearing one when nausea gas is used, you could choke on your puke. They're a drag to carry with you all the time. So a wet cloth spread over your nose and mouth is just as protective.

CN (weak) and CS (strong) come in canisters shot from guns, in grenades, and from helicopters. If you're going to throw canisters back at the pigs (you should) wear gloves because they are very hot. If you are tear gassed, splash lots of water into your eyes. Get to a fountain or open up a fire hydrant. If it's not too cold out, soak yourself entirely in water to wash all of the gas from your skin and clothes. You can also wipe the gas off with mineral oil or alcohol. But if you use water, use a lot; a little only makes it worse.

Nausea gas is shot in canisters. When it lands a little puff of smoke goes out and then nothing visible happens. It looks like a tear gas dud. But it ain't. The gas is totally odorless and colorless. So far it's been used rarely because in the streets anybody (including pigs) is vulnerable to it. If you're in a closed-off area, the possibility exists.

Blister gas is a powder. The pigs throw it into crowds after they've hosed the people with water. It burns the skin and lungs. Water makes it work, so more water doesn't help.

Mace is not a gas. It is a liquid the pig sprays from a can directly at your face. It causes heavy eye pain and can cause temporary blindness. Mace makes your breathing hard. You can wash your eyes

out with boric acid if you have it. It won't hurt less, but will be safety against eye infection.

Preparing Yourself

1. Get a tetanus shot. Tetanus is lockjaw. You can get it from lots of street injuries if you haven't been immunized in the last five years. You can get free tetanus shots from city health clinics or a movement doctor.

2. Know the address and phone number of the medical station near the staging area of each day's actions.

3. Wear a motorcycle helmet or surplus army helmet. Last year people got attacked for having helmets. That was because only a few people wore them. If we all wear a helmet, the pigs can't single one out for it. You protect everybody in the action by wearing a helmet. We got to prepare for what is coming down and not be scared of looking and acting like an army.

4. Wear protective clothing. Wear hard shoes, never wear sandals! Wear shirts and jackets with tight cuffs and high collars for protection against gas. Men should wear jock straps or cups. Women should wear bras. No one should wear earrings or anything around the neck. Get shatterproof glasses if you can

and strap all glasses around your head so they won't be knocked off. Do not wear contact lenses—they trap gasses in your eyes.

5. Don't carry scissors—you could be busted for carrying a concealed weapon.

6. If you have an illness that you know about, carry a card that tells about it, "I am a diabetic on insulin" or "I have penicillin allergy".

7. If you have to take some medicine regularly, you can take it into the streets. Keep it in a labelled descriptive bottle, or the pigs will bust you for dope and take the medicine. It's technically illegal for them to take labelled drugs, although that probably won't stop them.

8. Carry a magazine or rolled newspaper for a splint. Also carry a square foot of clean material for a bandage, a tourniquet, or a gas mask.

9. Everybody should carry (in an army belt or shoulder bag)

goggles for gas and mace protection

sterile 4 x 4 gauze pads to stop bleeding and cover nose and mouth

a roll of half-inch adhesive tape

some bandaids

a wet handkerchief

a plastic bag of wet cotton balls to rinse out eyes and wipe wounds

a small bottle of eyedrops

About Cars

The basic thing about cars is that most of the time they're more trouble than they're worth. The best thing to do when you arrive is to find some legal parking place in a residential area not too close to a movement center, and leave your car parked for the whole action unless it is absolutely necessary to use it. Cars with out-of-state plates and 10 freaks in them are always suspicious, even in normal situations. People with out-of-state licenses have to put up $25 in cash or sit in jail for any moving violation, such as things like a broken tail light. If people are arrested in a car, the car can be impounded. Tires of cars with out-of-state licenses are frequently slashed. Dope can be easily planted.

11. What are the underlying assumptions made by the writers of this article about the outcome of protest?
12. How does the advice given in the article, as well as the language used to express it, suggest that the differences between the protesters and the agents of the law are irreconcilable?
13. Explain the *irony* inherent in *Survival Kit*.
14. In your opinion, does *Survival Kit* point out the fact that law enforcement people should be disarmed? Or does it suggest that perhaps the protesters are not quite so blameless after all?
15. "I have to do what I truly feel is right." Which is the higher value, this one, or serving one's country?
16. Is this person's protest more effective than violence? Is it morally better than violent protest?

=======

Man must evolve for all human conflict a method which rejects revenge, aggression, and retaliation. The foundation of such a method is love.

Martin Luther King, accepting the Nobel Peace Prize, 1964.

=======

Canada: A Haven
For Cowards

by a veteran of the Korean War

Civil liberties groups, accompanied by various placard wavers and semi-professional protesters, have all condemned what they term the "inhumane" treatment afforded the refugee from military service.

They defend, specifically, the American draft dodger or deserter who states he came to Canada on a matter of principle, conveniently labelled "anti-Vietnam," and adopts the title of political refugee.

Political refugees have been, historically, the types who left their homeland only when they could do no more to change the system from within, generally after years of effort which had made their position untenable.

They leave to continue the fight from somewhere else, a country which, in most cases, has a differing political background from their own. A Russian, fleeing Communist ideology, does not choose China for asylum.

The draft dodger or deserter does not leave the US because of persecution, discrimination, poverty, coercion or disreputable behaviour by persons highly placed.

He does not leave a graft-ridden society for cleaner air.

He rarely leaves for economic reasons.

He leaves simply because he does not wish to go to war.

That is the beginning of the end.

Man can live alone, and survive. The instant he relinquishes some of this sovereignty he becomes human instead of animal, and multiplied by the thousands he becomes a nation, with responsibilities.

To run from this responsibility, he detracts from his humanity and multiplied by thousands, he again becomes animal.

Most governments recognize the conscientious objector— the man to whom fighting is completely out of the question. In the main, these people have lived this type of life since birth. A conscientious objector is not someone who suddenly decides he would like to be one because it is to his advantage.

Nothing but admiration is due a person who does not wish to participate in killing in any fashion, and will fight his own fight on the existing battle-ground—within his own country.

But to run when there is a chance to present an objective criticism labels the deserter as a hypocrite and coward.

This type of person will no more defend Canada than the country of his birth, as he will find that many of the reasons he left the United States exist here as well, including a reasonable and honorable request to defend the principles of its existence.

The draft dodger is not a glamorous rebel, but a running, frightened coward, and the world has seen many of these.

A parasite is a parasite.

. . . in all activist situations there is likely to develop what we know familiarly as the "we-and-they" mentality, where "they" become, from the students' point of view, something authoritarian and established and to be described in solid metaphors. That is, the establishment is a structure, and however much corroded with dry rot and the death watch beetle, however near to collapse it may be, it is still to be thought of as something solidified and frozen. On the other hand, the freedom of the individual is associated with liquid metaphors, of getting things stirred up and the like. Neither of these metaphors really covers, of course, the situation they are describing.

Professor Northrop Frye
on student protest

The remarkable phenomenon of student opposition was due to several factors, chief among them what so many people call sneeringly "the revolt of modern youth." Now this revolt, which involves ever larger numbers of young people through the world, must not be confused with the old "conflict between the generations." The latter, as we know it, particularly in earlier forms of bourgeois society, reflected the impatience of the young to step into the shoes of the old. This impatience often took the form of an attack on the fossilized thinking of the older generation and sometimes crystallized into a liberal, radical or a reformist attitude. In the current revolt of youth, however, very much more is being questioned—the distaste is for the system itself. Modern youth is not so much envious of, as disgusted with, the dead, empty lives of their parents. This feeling began among bourgeois children but has now spread through all levels of society. Daniel Mothé (*Socialisme ou Barbarie* No. 33) has shown clearly how opposed young workers are to both the "values" that capitalist society has to offer them and also to working class values and traditional forms of organization (political parties and trade unions). Factory work, trade union "militancy", verbose party programmes, and the sad, colourless life of their elders are subjects only for their sarcasm and contempt.

The same sort of disdain is the reason why so many students have taken a radical stand, and have made common cause with young workers in the struggle against a repressive society.

Daniel Cohn-Bendit,
student activist

17a. Show how the language used by Daniel Cohn-Bendit and by the Korean War veteran reflect the "we-they" mentality described by Professor Frye.
  b. Are the two attitudes irreconcilable?
18. Examine the two opposing articles carefully, and note the points at which each writer makes personal assumptions.

THINK

(a) "In certain ways, young people—especially high school and university students—are no different from the Fascists under Hitler and Mussolini. They listen with their hearts and not their heads, to the people they want to hear, and anyone else is shouted down in a typically anti-mind, mob-like Fascist manner." Is there some truth to this statement?

(b) Why is most of the protest in our society carried out by young people?

(c) "Most protesters are either 'jumping on a bandwagon,' since protest is popular, or else they are seeking some form of selfish material gain. Then too, some of them are merely trying to get back at their parents in a very immature way." Do you agree with any of the above claims?

(d) "I've said [to students]: 'What you want is more life. What you want is to be alive. You protest in the name of life.' They know exactly what I'm talking about." (Erich Fromm) *Exactly* what is he talking about?

(e) Of what value are the protests by people like Jan Palyk (immolated himself in Czechoslovakia in protest against the Russian occupation)?

(f) Resolved: That any man has the right to protect himself from violence by any means at his disposal.
  Resolved: That since man cannot change, it is logical to try to change the system.

(g) Form groups to discuss the extent to which you would impose rules of behaviour and dress if you were running your school. What forms of protest would you allow?

(h) Is there an inherent flaw in each of the following statements?

    i. Guns don't kill. People do.

    ii. Since western society has traditionally used violent dissent to bring about constitutional change, e.g. Peterloo, Boston Tea Party, French Revolution, Riel Rebellion, it is both normal and natural to expect—in fact invite—violence from the people.

    iii. In any nation, the silent majority which does not actively protest war, or injustice, or racism, is, in fact, condoning these practices.

    iv. Roman emperors recognized the natural tendencies toward violence in their citizens and appeased them with bloody, violent spectacles. Perhaps modern rulers should do the same.

7. RELIGION

Why Christians And Atheists Find They Have A Great Deal In Common

by *Wayne Edmondstone*

Christians should be prepared to listen to atheists and possibly to learn from them as well, a priest suggests.

Rev. Arthur Gibson, professor of religious studies at St. Michael's College, put forward the somewhat startling idea on a recent television program called Faith of an Atheist.

Such a suggestion may appear to be a radical departure from the traditional Christian urge to "convert" non-believers—an attitude still widely held, particularly amongst the more fundamentalist denominations—but it is typical of the increasing tendency of churches in general to attempt to understand the beliefs of others in comparison to their own.

In fact, Christians have been "listening" to a number of professed atheists for years and, although there have been remarkably few conversions on either side, both factions are beginning to realize that they have a great deal in common.

One Roman Catholic philosopher, the French Jesuit

Teilhard de Chardin, went so far as to suggest that both the man of religious vocation and the atheist were absolutely essential; that each needed the opinions and attitudes of the other in order to discover truth.

For although they differ in their attitudes towards the necessity of a belief in a higher power, the Christian and the atheist are united in their common concern for the condition of man.

From the Christian point of view, the most popular of the contemporary atheists—and the one most consistently quoted in sermons—is the late French author and philosopher, Albert Camus, a profoundly religious man who did not believe in God.

The man who loves life, Camus argued, is forced to attempt to improve it for others. He must fight the evils of death, sickness, ignorance and poverty even though he knows, because of his own mortality, that he will never be completely successful.

Belief in all-powerful God weakens man's desire to eradicate the ills and injustices of life, because in moments of severe tension he may simply give up the fight and leave the solution to his creator, Camus argued.

Yet in a 1948 address to a Dominican order near Paris, this man, who had a profound respect for the moral values of Christianity, begged Christians to unite with unbelievers for the good of man.

And despite his lack of belief he continued to advocate dialogue between the two groups until his death in 1960.

Another atheist who has exercised a considerable influence on contemporary Christianity is the ubiquitous Jean-Paul Sartre.

An author, playwright and existentialist philosopher, Sartre, like his countryman Camus, sees life as essentially absurd and religion as meaningless superstition.

Yet his outlook towards individual responsibility is shared by large numbers of "Christian Existentialists."

"We have lost 'religion'—in the traditional sense of the word—but have gained humanism," he asserts. "The ideal now is to liberate and help emancipate mankind, with the result that man becomes really an absolute for man."

Put more simply, Sartre's basic premise is that man is not just an automation to be manipulated by "divine will" (benevolent or otherwise) but a free agent who governs his life through his own conscious choices.

But although he keeps insisting that God is dead, Sartre has resolutely refused to substitute man for Him and cynically insists that man is merely another creature "who aspires to be God."

Not everyone agrees with this self-assessment. Critic Frank Kappler says of Sartre: "Having found there is no God and no life after death, and having none-the-less opted for an *engagement* for the common benefit of mankind, he may now suffer the supreme indignity of being told 'You, in the most real sense, are truly religious.' "

Perhaps the most recent atheistic philosopher to capture the fancy of Christendom is Romanian-born E. M. Cioran, a 58-year-old recluse who lives in Paris.

Little known in North America but widely respected in Europe, Cioran, more than any other contemporary thinker, has stated the case for total pessimism as he rails against the lack of challenging intellect in contemporary Christian thinking.

"Christianity no longer inconveniences the mind nor enforces the least interrogation; the anxieties it provokes, like its answers and its solutions, are flabby, soporific. Already we yawn over the cross," he writes.

Despite his assertion that he believes in "nothing;" ("For me, life is a passionate emptiness, an intriguing nothingness.") Cioran makes the startling admission that he cannot totally reject the idea of a supreme being.

If Christians choose to follow the lead suggested by Father Gibson and listen to such men as these, they will undoubtedly be angered and hurt by much of what they hear.

But at the same time they will learn the hopes and agonies of those without faith, whose ranks—by the churches' own admission—would appear to be growing day by day.

1. What does "being religious" mean to you? Is it possible to be religious without believing in God?
2. Is an atheist as disposed to helping his fellow man as someone who believes in God? Is an agnostic?

3. Can an atheist be as fulfilled as one who believes in God?
4. According to Rev. Gibson, what do Christians have to gain by dialogue with atheists?

Experiencing God is the highest high, the ultimate trip.

seminarian

Religion And World History

by W. W. Bauer

In practically every culture, we find a belief in some form of supernatural influence upon man and his world. Thor, the thunder god of the Norsemen; the Manitou, the Great Spirit of the American Indian; Isis and Osiris, the chief gods of the Egyptians; the moon deity Nannar of Sumerian Ur; the bearded "fair god" Quetzalcoatl of the Mexican Toltecs and the sungod pyramids of the Aztecs; all are examples which show not only the diversity but the similarity of religious belief as an explanation for the world and its mysteries. In India, there was born the Brahman belief, centered about a trinity—Brahma, the Creator of the Universe, Vishna, its preserver, and Siva, who represents both destruction and reproduction. The Greeks created a whole galaxy of gods and goddesses, many of them endowed with attributes anything but admirable, and the Romans adopted them, with variations. Roman theology finally descended to the low level of emperor deification, including some characters like Caligula, whom a schoolboy unwittingly characterized with great accuracy when asked to write an essay about him. He had not studied his lesson, but he was not stupid. He wrote: "The less said, the better!"

The diversity of these beliefs, and others, is striking, but there is also a strong thread of similarity. In all theologies, the gods were represented as creators, benefactors, controllers, avengers and destroyers. They were concerned with life, death, illness, misfortune, good fortune, love, reproduction, virtue, and wickedness. In the Egyptian world of the dead and the American Indian's happy hunting ground there is indication of a single basic origin. Indeed, the Braham trinity, the father-mother gods of the Egyptians and the Christian Trinity are among the many indications which have led both theologians and scientists to conclude that man's original religion was monotheistic, a belief in one God, Creator and Ruler of the universe. The Judaic Scriptures, which tell of the dispersion of man as a punishment for aspiring to the status of deity when he built the tower in the plain of Babel, are cited as the beginning of diversities in religious belief.

Any scrutiny of early beliefs in the closely related areas of religion, myth, magic and medicine show the strong trend toward personalizing natural phenomena such as sun, moon, stars, earth, sea, clouds, rain, thunder, lightning, plants, animals, springs, rivers, and mountains.

5a. According to Bauer, why have so many different civilizations developed similar religious beliefs and practices?
  b. Is his point an adequate explanation for the existence of religion?
  c. Do you agree that this passage implies that belief in deities is born of ignorance?

I think we believe in God because we're scared. I mean, we don't know things like what actually started evolution, so we believe in God just to be sure.

Brad M., 10 years old

There are some who scoff at the Bible, and at stories such as Noah and the Ark. They might do well to consider these . . .
— Sumerian legend has it that the god Enki warned the pious king Ziusudra of a flood that was to wipe out the human race, and Ziusudra saved himself by using a boat.
— Babylon tells of the gods decreeing destruction of mankind by flood, but the god Ea warned Utnapishtim who built a boat for his family and animals and was saved. When the boat came to rest on Mount Nisii, Utnapishtim sent out a swallow, and a raven before he was certain the ground was dry.
— The Hittites had a similar account.
— So do the Egyptians.
— A boat-shaped scar, roughly corresponding to the size of the Ark has been photographed on the side of Mount Ararat.
— Fragments of wood, carbon-dated as at least 4,000 years old, have been discovered on Ararat, well above the tree line . . . .

* * *

6. What are some other passages from the Bible that have similar accounts in the history and legends of non-Judao-Christian peoples?
7. Does the fusion of legend with Judao-Christian belief weaken the latter?

Religion Is The Extra Dimension

by Most Rev. Philip Hannan, Roman Catholic Archbishop

Does religion have a future? The answer depends on the answer to another question: Does man have a future?

Religion is not something set apart from man. More than doctrines, laws and institutions, religion is the living relationship between man and God. As long as this relationship endures, religion will have not just a future but a central role in human life.

How much does man need God now? For the believer, the obvious answer is—at least as much as before and quite possibly more than ever. But not everyone accepts this. We are told God is "dead," that modern man has passed beyond the stage of needing God, that therefore man does not stand in need of religion anymore.

It is not hard to see why some people think this way. The superstitious "need" for God and religion has long since passed. We no longer invoke mysterious powers to bring rain or cause crops to grow. We understand the natural processes involved and with increasing skills we are able to control them ourselves.

We can do even more marvelous things in the fields of communication, transportation, medicine and biology. Yet none of these developments truly challenges religion. Every advance of modern science and technology, if seen in proper perspective, represents part of man's working out of the mission given him by God: to draw out and perfect the powers latent in the material universe and, especially, in the mind of man himself.

God does not expect us to be superstitious peasants blindly placating the mysterious powers of nature. God has made us human beings with eager, inquiring minds and amazing talents of discovery and invention. In uncovering the powers within the universe and within ourselves, we are doing what God expects of us and performing a truly religious act.

Yet it is painfully clear that not every scientific discovery and technical advance has been utilized for the good. This is

all too obvious in an age when mankind lives under the threat of nuclear annihilation. On this score, too, religion has some thing vital to say to modern man.

It is simply this: The fact that man *can* do something does not mean that he *should* do it. Whether something can be done is one question; whether it ought to be done is a very different question—one that scientific knowledge and technical skill are unable to answer by themselves.

Thus, one of the main tasks of religion remains now—as it has been in the past and will be in the future—to guide man in making choices about the kind of world he will shape for himself. Today we have the knowledge and technical skill to solve such age-old problems as war, poverty, sickness and discrimination. But whether we will do so does not in the last analysis depend on our knowledge and our technical skill but upon our sense of what we *ought* to do. And to grasp what we ought to do, we must look to religion.

For it is religion that helps man understand what it means to be fully human. Religion adds the extra dimension to human life that distinguishes it from brute existence on the one hand and machine-like impersonality on the other. Religion does something else. Equally important, it is the framework within which man works out his relationship with God Himself.

The more man pushes back the frontiers of his own knowledge and skill, the more aware he becomes that the ultimate riddles of human life are beyond his unaided solution. The power to split the atom does not explain how an atom came to be. The ability to decipher the genetic code does not tell how a unique human life came into existence. Man's most striking discoveries only reinforce the conclusion that man must seek the answer to the meaning of his life somewhere beyond himself—in God.

Organized religion has made many mistakes. It will certainly make many more. Sometimes it has seemed so remote from human affairs as to be scarcely relevant to man. At other times it has been so immersed in the world that it has appeared to be merely one more power system or, in a more favorable perspective, one more humanitarian movement. Religion needs to balance both elements—humanizing human life, while giving constant witness to the God who transcends human life. Man needs both and will continue to need both in the future.

Is there a future for religion? As long as there is for man.

8. Compare the explanation of religion given by Archbishop Hannan, with *humanism*.

9. When the United States suffered the first setback in its space exploration program in 1970, people the world over prayed for the safe return of the astronauts whose lives were in danger. What is the meaning and purpose of prayer?

Tradition And Meaning

by Chaim Potok

In the cold December time of the year, when the sun appears about to be snuffed out by an encroaching darkness and a weariness of the flesh and spirit begins to set in, Jews celebrate the Festival of Lights. For eight consecutive days, candles are lighted in the windows of Jewish homes throughout the world. These are the Eight Days of Dedication—Hanukkah, they are called in Hebrew—a time when it is remembered what a zealous few were once able to accomplish against the might of an empire.

Picture a land about 35 miles long and between 25 and 30 miles broad, much of it desert, a land that contained a single city: Jerusalem. This was the district of Judea, the nation of the Jews, a tiny portion of the vast Asiatic empire of the Seleucids.

In the month of December, 167 years before the birth of Jesus, Antiochus IV, who was King of Syria and therefore ruler of the Jews, abrogated the law of Moses, made the observance of Jewish ritual an act punishable by death, decreed that the Temple in Jerusalem be used for idolatry, and ordered the Jews of Judea to worship the gods of the pagans.

One year later, agents of the King entered Modin, a town along the road from Jaffa to Jerusalem, to oversee a pagan sacrifice. A Jew stepped forward ready to perform the sacrifice. Another Jew, Mattathias, slew him and one of the agents as well. Then, with his five sons, he fled into the hills of Judea, where others soon joined him. The revolution had begun.

It lasted about 32 years before Judea won its independence. Sometime during that period, Jerusalem was captured by the rebels and the Temple rededicated to the worship of God. It is the rededication of the Temple that is celebrated by the candles of Hanukkah.

All through the centuries, Jews have lighted those candles—
in wanderings, in persecutions, amidst the blood and hate that
surrounded them. And they light them today, too, everywhere.

Now, in a world where God is proclaimed to be dead and
the young search valiantly for new values, in a time of a sub-
culture of rock and pot and a hunger for simple love between
human beings, in a period of disillusionment with mouthed
moralities—in such a world, how insignificant that ancient
revolution must appear, how absurd the candles that celebrate
it.

But it will continue to be celebrated. The candles will continue to be lighted. And the wise among the young will learn
quickly enough that in a world of violent change there must
be certain anchors to the past.

The revolution begun on a distant strip of land more than
2,000 years ago is one such anchor. It was fought by men who
felt that war was hateful but that a tyranny that strangles
the soul of a people was more hateful. Had they lost that war,
Judaism would probably have been obliterated and Christianity
would not have been born—and the love and the values and
the simple human decencies for which the young now hunger
and which they see uttered in words and ignored in acts, these
would never have become the heritage of Western man.

Sometimes one is led to believe that the world continues to
exist by virtue of the small good things that go on despite the
pain and the ugliness that surround us, and that violence itself
is possible only against a background of tiny, anchored nor-
malcies. If all was violence, the world would disintegrate.

The candles of Hanukkah are small good things in the wide
darkness of our December nights.

10a. How has our world benefitted from the traditions and rituals
of religion?
  b. What are the effects of religious ritual on an individual?

The Twenty-fifth of December

by Raymond Souster

Pile the windows high
till they almost crack,
heap the monumental
Junkpile of Christmas,
forty-nine price tags
and a picture of Santa Claus,
fifty-nine price tags
and a barber-pole candy-cane,
hark the herald angels
sing all sales final,
peace on earth and mercy
to all cash customers,
O little town of Bethlehem
ONLY TWO SHOPPING DAYS
Noel, Noel,
scotch pines $2.50,
sixty-nine price tags
and a tinsel-coloured sky,
Good King Wenceslas
in the bargain basement . . . .

Merry Christmas ·
suckers.

But What Are The Young People Doing?

Whether young people are the most important group in our society or not, certainly they get the most publicity. And their part in the "failing-church" syndrome is no exception. Every investigation into the declining attendance rates at church ultimately comes to the conclusion that organized religion is suffering from arteriosclerosis, that young people are no longer interested in the religious practices of their parents, and that the survival of any church in the twentieth century depends upon a complete overthrow of the old ways.

The first question that older people ask is "Why? What gives *this* generation a supposed insight that no other has had?" Some of the answers are obvious. Younger people seem to be engaged in a thoroughgoing rejection of everything that their parents believed in. Since organized religion has always been one of the pillars in that body of belief, it is natural to assume that it will be among the first to fall.

Other factors, too, enter into this abandonment of the traditional forms. A basic tenet of religion has always been the promise of future reward, achieved in part by outward acts of worship. For young people raised in the shadow of The Bomb, and The Cold War, there is no future; there is only now, the present. And for them, outward acts are often the antithesis to what they feel is inward hypocrisy. It seems that young people will not accept a pattern of life that piles up treasure on earth for five days a week, rests on them on Saturday, and then for an hour on Sunday, piles up treasures in heaven.

Revelations in science have disturbed much of the comfort supplied by religion. Rapid communications have made obvious what man is capable of doing to his fellow man. Improved, or at least more honest, education systems no longer teach history in terms of right and wrong. Students today realize, for example, that the Crusaders were probably more guilty of crimes against God than the Moslems were.

But because young people are turning from organized religion, this does not mean, axiomatically, that they are not *religious*. According to many psychologists and social philosophers, the young are desperately sacramental, seeking through physical means the saving meaning that they can no longer get from the traditional ways. The Be-in, sensitivity groups, emotive dancing in close group contact, terribly loud music that puts everyone on the same emotional wave length, even pot parties—all these are replacing the ritual and meaning of organized religion. By means that shock and sometimes horrify their parents, young people seem to be anxiously searching for a religion that will *re*-humanize man in the present technological age. In their search lies the most likely solution for those who worry about the future of organized religion.

Instead of private worship, young people want public action. Clearing a polluted river, walking twenty miles for charity, feeding a hungry nation—these acts, to youth, are more religious than the most solemn of rituals. Whereas dogma and canon law have hitherto provided the guidelines for right and wrong, the individual conscience and love must now become the backbone of religion. Prayers on the gold-edged pages of leather-bound books are no longer adequate; prayers are now written on placards of civil rights protesters. Young people do not see Jesus Christ, or Mohammed, or any great religious figure for that matter, as meek and mild. They see Christ as a revolutionary who was not afraid to step on the toes of the Establishment. Only those churches that take the same stance are going to survive.

11. According to this article, do the actions of the young indicate a deteriorating or a strengthening belief in God?
12. In your opinion, has the writer missed any important points that explain why fewer young people attend church?
13. Can a religion exist without dogma, without organization?

God Is For Real, Man

by Rev. Carl Burke

They was a rich guy who had two sons. Junior says, "Hey, Dad, how's about giving me my share of your dough now, why wait until you kick off?"

His father says, "OK, man," and gave him half his money. So Junior starts off to have a good time. At first, he's got lots of friends, a white Cadillac, two suits, and what he eats is real class, and beer at every meal. But, pretty soon the money is all gone and he's dead broke.

So he's got no friends, no money, no nothin'; and, man, oh man, is he hungry, and no pad to sleep in. He goes over to the stockyards to look for a job, and gets one feeding the pigs. The boss don't pay very much, and the pigs get more food than he does.

So Junior thinks this over and says, "I must be some kind of a nut. I was better off at home. It wasn't so bad at that. I guess I'll go home and tell 'em I'm sorry I made a real goof of this one."

All the time this is goin' on, Dad's thinkin' about it, too. He's plenty worried about Junior getting mixed up with queers and winos and he wishes that Junior would come home. So he watches out the window every night.

Then one day he sees Junior way down the end of the long block. Dad runs like crazy to meet him. Junior starts to tell his dad how sorry he is and that he made a goof to do what he did. But his dad tells him to knock it off and come home and get some clean rags on and we'll have a big supper. Dad's pretty happy to see the little cat 'cause he thought that Junior was dead, and that he would never see him again.

While this was happenin', the other son had stayed home and worked. He was out workin' his paper route when Junior came home. When he gets home from his papers he sees a wild party. So he says, "What gives?" Some guy says, "Your brother came home, and your dad's throwin' a party." This makes him mad, and he says, "To hell with that jazz," and won't even go in the house.

Dad comes out and tries to talk him into it. He says, "I stay home and sell papers and keep this place clean, and you don't buy me a damn thing. Junior here chickens out on his big plans and you throw a party and say 'Glad to see you home.' Well, I say to hell with him."

The old man's not so dumb and gets on to what happens here and knows that he just jealous. So he says, "My boy, you just settle down a minute. I thought he was a gone cat and was dead, but he ain't and I'm happy. I could always see you but him I couldn't. This party is for me, I'm so happy." That's how God feels when people come back to him.

14. Carl Burke prepared this book when he was chaplain of Erie County Jail in New York. Young people for whom the Bible had little meaning rewrote it in their own idiom. Is this story of the Prodigal Son less religious than the King James or any other accepted version? Is it accurate? Does it have meaning?

The New-Time Religion

by Rev. Robert Raines,
First Methodist Church, Philadelphia

Recently, in a fashionable Protestant church, the four ushers put the offering plates on the altar and turned to walk to the rear of the church. The first two were young men in their thirties, both with gorgeous, bushy mustaches. The second two were lovely teen-age girls in mini-skirts. Nobody arranged for the mustaches and mini-skirts that morning. It just happened that way.

Thirty years ago in that church the ushers were invariably older men, pillars of substance and dignity, and wore tails. The recent policy of occasionally using mini-skirted girls as ushers has been met with consternation by some and delight by others. Obviously, something significant, some would say drastic, has happened in that congregation and others across the country. The mood has shifted from solemnity to celebration.

For example, instead of the traditional pastoral prayer, a minister or layman may stand up in the midst of the congregation, ask the people to express their concerns, listen to them, and then offer up the prayers of the congregation as they have been expressed. All through the service the emphasis is on participation by the people instead of a performance by the minister. Instead of the traditional sermon, there may be a short story written by a member of the congregation, slides or a short film, a dialogue or drama. Instead of the traditional music, there may be pop songs—the Beatles as well as Bach, guitars as well as an organ, dance as well as the doxology.

At the present time this swinging style prevails in a small minority of congregations across the country, but it has the feel and face of the future. A new-time religion is breaking out, and with it congregations are breaking up. Not every one favors the changes. Some churches virtually split into two congregations, embodying the generation gap. It's a disturbing time of conflict and change. But the new-time religion is tapping and releasing emotional power after decades of dead worship. And, most important, this emotional power is being matched by intellectual inquiry and social involvement. Many ministers, laymen and congregations are deeply involved in the issues of racism, Vietnam and poverty.

Opinions on such issues differ drastically. But it is clear that many people who had given up on the church as hopelessly reactionary and dull (which, for the most part, it still is) are taking a second look at churches where concerned involvement is manifest. Lots of these new-lookers are young. The new-lookers don't intend to leave things to the officials, but want to help change things themselves. They are taking the wraps off a gentle Jesus meek and mild, smelling flowers or carrying lambs, to discover a tough young man who associated with the poor and outcasts of his day, flayed the religious establishment for its hypocrisy and injustice, broke sacred religious laws again and again in order to serve human need, and put on a smashing one-man demonstration in the most influential cathedral of the nation to protest its exploitation of the faithful.

Jesus can't be put in stained glass anymore. He isn't dead, but alive and well, stirring things up on the streets and in the churches. He's bringing in, not the sheaves, but the revolution of human freedom and justice. He's controversial, as will be congregations that take him seriously.

The new-time religion is not only activist—religion without action is worth precisely nothing—but reflective. Its adherents seek insight and friendship, prayer, and play. There is a theological openness and modesty in growing numbers of congregations, the recognition, as it was put by the late James Pike, that we need "fewer beliefs and more belief." There is room for doubt and diversity. Dogma is out, dialogue and discussion are in. There is the recognition of mystery, and that the revelations of God are many.

In our computerized society people are hungry to know and be known face-to-face. Many congregations provide an opportunity for small groups of people to meet in homes, offices and apartments to share their concerns, questions and hopes. Many find deeper friendship and insight than conventional social gatherings afford.

I have described the creative minority in the church today. If this minority were to grow, and eventually become the prevailing style of Christianity, significant results would occur.

1. Young people who are seeking authentic community, meaning, justice, truth, but are now turned off by the hypocrisy and irrelevance of the church, would try out the church again.

2. The institutional church would shrink radically. There would be fewer church buildings, bureaucrats, congregations, members, clergymen and dollars. In their place would come new lay ministries and small congregations gathering in homes around issues of common concern.

3. Christianity would present a life-style that confronts the prevailing culture rather than, as is the case now, conforms to it—with the result that both the cost and joy of being a Christian would be considerably magnified.

4. The church would be free to become a community of searching celebrators with an openness, courage, honesty, compassion and joy that it hasn't been since the first century.

15. In your opinion, are the attitudes and actions of the "New-Time" religion less God-oriented than the old ways?
16. Show how the general organization, sentence structure, diction, allusions, and other features of this passage, subtly downgrade the traditional aspects of religious practice.

THINK

(a) $Ff^2(MgE)—C^1Ri^1xM=L/So$
or put in simpler terms:
. . . The number of stars in the Universe is so infinite that if only *one in a billion* is a sun with planets . . .
. . . and if only *one in a billion* of all these planets is of Earth size and composition . . .
. . . the Universe would still contain approximately 2,800,-000,000,000,000,000,000,000,000,000 planets capable of supporting oxygen-carbon life, just as Earth does. Does this equation support or refute the belief that God exists?
(b) Resolved: That religion is a comfort.

(c) Resolved: That Jesus Christ, by twentieth-century standards of behaviour, was a radical.

(d) Resolved: That both Jewish and Christian theology support violence if it will bring about justice.

(e) If civilization as we know it, should collapse, would this mean the end of religion?

(f) What is your concept of God? Of heaven? Of hell?

(g) Do all religions have a heaven and a hell?

(h) For investigation:

    i. the philosophy of yoga

    ii. I Ching (sometimes called *The Book of Changes*)

    iii. Nichiren Shoshu

    iv. cloistered communities

    v. Taoism

8. GENERATION

A friend of mine pleasantly asked a sixteen-year-old girl why she was wearing a decorative bell hung around her neck on a long leather thong: "Is that so your mother knows where you're at?'
She answered just as pleasantly: That's so I know where *I'm* at."

from *The Gap,*
by Lorber and Fladell

Today's Youth

by Kenneth Keniston

We often feel that today's youth are somehow "different." There is something about today's world that seems to give the young a special restlessness, an increased impatience with the "hypocrisies" of the past, and yet an open gentleness and a searching honesty more intense than that of youth in the past. Much of what we see in today's students and non-students is, of course, familiar: to be young is, in one sense, always the same. But it is also new and different, as each generation confronts its unique historical position and role.

Yet we find it hard to define the difference. Partly the difficulty derives from the elusive nature of youth itself. Still, this generation seems even more elusive than most—and that, too, may be one of the differences. Partly the problem stems from the sheer variety and number of "youth" in a society where youth is often protracted into the mid-twenties. No one characterization can be adequate to the drop-outs and stay-ins, hawks and doves, up-tights and cools, radicals and conservatives, heads and seekers that constitute American youth. But although we understand that the young are as various as the old in our complex society, the sense that they are different persists.

In giving today's American youth this special quality and mood, two movements have played a major role: the New Left and the hippies. Both groups are spontaneous creations of the young; both are in strong reaction to what Paul Goodman calls the Organized System; both seek alternatives to the institutions of middle-class life. Radicals and hippies are also different from each other in numerous ways, from psychodynamics to ideology. The hippie has dropped out of a society he considers irredeemable: his attention is riveted on interior change and the expansion of personal consciousness. The radical has not given up on this society: his efforts are aimed at changing and redeeming it. Furthermore, both "movements" together comprise but a few percent of their contemporaries, But, although neither hippies nor New Leftists are "representative" of their generation, together they are helping to give this generation its distinctive mood. By examining the style of these young men and women, we come closer to understanding what makes their generation "different."

* * *

Post-modern youth views itself primarily as a part of a generation rather than an organization; they identify with their contemporaries as a group, rather than with elders; and they do not have clearly defined leaders and heroes. Their deepest collective identification is to their own group or "Movement"—

a term that in its ambiguous meanings points not only to the fluidity and openness of post-modern youth, but to its physical mobility, and the absence of traditional patterns of leadership and emulation. Among young radicals, for example, the absence of heroes or older leaders is impressive: even those five years older are sometimes viewed with mild amusement or suspicion. And although post-modern youth is often widely read in the "literature" of the New Left or that of consciousness-expansion, no one person or set of people is central to their intellectual beliefs. Although they live together in groups, these groups are without clear leaders.

Generational consciousness also entails a feeling of psychological disconnection from previous generations, their life situations and their ideologies. Among young radicals there is a strong feeling that the older ideologies are exhausted or irrelevant, expressed in detached amusement at the doctrinaire disputes of the "old Left" and impatience with "old liberals." Among hippies, the irrelevance of the parental past is even greater: if there is any source of insight, it is the timeless tradition of the East, not the values of the previous generation in American society. But in both groups, the central values are those created in the present by the "Movement" itself.

1a. What are some of the " 'hypocrisies' of the past" to which today's youth objects?
 b. Why has no youthful generation rejected them before this?
2. How have the New Left and the hippies influenced youth today?
3. A prominent North American figure has said that today's youth are anti-everything and pro-nothing. What answer does this article give to that statement? What evidence in the behaviour of youth would support such a statement?
4. In spite of the article's contention that today's young people have no heroes, several people have emerged in the last several years who might qualify as heroes for youth. Who are some of these people? What qualities made them *heroes?*

Telling Lies To The Young Is Wrong

by Yevgeny Yevtushenko

Telling lies to the young is wrong.
Proving to them that lies are true is wrong.
Telling them that God's in his heaven
and all's well with the world is wrong.
The young know what you mean.
The young are people.
Tell them the difficulties can't be counted,
and let them see not only what will be
but see with clarity these present times.
Say obstacles exist they must encounter,
sorrow happens, hardship happens.
The hell with it. Who never knew
the price of happiness will not be happy.
Forgive no error you recognise,
it will repeat itself, increase,
and afterwards our pupils
will not forgive in us what we forgave.

5. On which side of the generation gap does this poem belong?

It [youthful criticism of big business] shows . . . an indifference to—even an unawareness of—the lessons of history, a narrow focusing on the present to the exclusion of the past and the future, and an apparent failure to comprehend the social and psychological forces that determine how societies and organizations function and change. And all of this is combined with what often seems to be grossly distorted perceptions of present-day reality.

R. S. Ritchie,
vice-president of Imperial Oil

6a. What are the benefits of being able to view the present day in the light of the past? Are there any disadvantages?
  b. In what way is the last sentence of Mr. Ritchie's statement symbolic of the "generation gap"?
7a. What are the dangers of looking at things from the present only, and from one's own point of view only?
  b. Do you agree that young people see only the present?

The Gap

by Lorber and Fladell

The Gap *is the result of a collaboration between a twenty-year-old student (Richie) and his forty-two-year-old uncle (Ernie). What follows is a few selected passages.*

Richie (having just introduced his uncle to pot):

"As I reflect upon what I have written I realize something that may be obvious. I introduced Ernie to pot, I turned him on, and I wanted him to get high. But now that he claims to know the experience I feel somewhat resentful; it is as if he had crashed a very private party I was having with myself. I can no longer condescend to him about the mysteries of pot; my cultural insularity burned away in his throat."

*   *   *

Ernie:

"I also became aware that these kids don't often use terms like "blowing your cool," "up tight," "groovy," expressions you find in profusion in slick magazines and advertisements that pretend to be on the inside of the youth scene. Richie and his friends seem to be very studied in their refusal to talk the language they are supposed to talk. And so at about the time they think you know what they are saying, they have changed the words and the meanings.

About this matter of language, Richie says that one of the big problems between generations is that we don't think the same things are funny. And I'll admit so far my experiences with Richie haven't been exactly a barrel of laughs, although he may be having one or two privately."

*   *   *

Ernie:

". . . I realized that my credits as the president of a small advertising agency had preceded me. There was nothing much more about that for a while, and then one of the kids asked me point-blank how come I don't do a clever ad for peace in Vietnam. I said I would be glad to if anyone asked me to and paid me for it, although I would like it to run in the Peking Express as well as The New York Times.

Then somebody said, "Would you take the Dow account?"

"You bet," I said.

"Even though they make napalm?" he asked.

I asked him how he was going to school and who was paying for it. "My father's bosses' money," he answered.

"Supposing your father worked for Dow selling Saran Wrap. Would that mean that you would quit school in protest?"

One of the other kids said: "Oh! that's hardly fair."

But another one said it was so fair and somehow in the ensuing discussion I got off the hook for a while.

Then someone asked me if I was defensive about advertising and I said "No, only when I allow my agency to do bad advertising." I was pushed rather hard on that one and for the only time that evening I tried to get through to them by trying to explain my interest in doing good work. I thought I was making some points by telling them of the new graphics and copy approach we use and how we try to tell it true and then somebody said "But what you're saying is that you're working within the system and trying to improve it. And what we're saying is that the system shouldn't exist at all."

I would have asked him what he wanted to replace with it, but somehow I knew he really had no ideas on that subject. I asked Richie about him later and he explained that this boy was completely apolitical, or rather that he practiced politics of the perverse. Whatever that means.

During most of the conversation I was careful not to say too much or overexplain or be too defensive. I initiated nothing and tried to answer the questions that were put to me with a "yes" or "no" wherever possible.

At one point a kid asked me: "Why did you go into advertising in the first place?"

I thought back almost twenty years and answered as honestly as I could: 'To make a living.'

He then said: "That's one of the things I can't understand about you fellows, doing what you do just to make a lot of money.'

I said: 'I went into advertising to make a living, not to make a lot of money.' Even as I said it I knew the phrase to *make a living* could have absolutely no meaning to these children of the affluent society."

*　　*　　*

Richie:

". . . there seems to be an intense conceit among middle-aged people about the very fact that they have had more experience than the so-called younger generation. Without a thought for the variety and quality of experience (refusing to consider the differences between their experiences and their children's), they can only think in terms of the quantity of experience and demand respect for the authority of age with no reasons given. Does the oldest person always have to be the wisest person?"

*　　*　　*

8. Some readers of these passages have said that the personal reflections of Richie and Ernie show that the older and younger generations are jealous of each other. Do you agree?

The judge shall not be young; he should have learned to know evil, not from his own soul, but from late and long observation of the nature of evil in others.

Plato

The Trouble With Parents

from a discussion by young people conducted by Sylvie Reice for McCall's Magazine

We decided then to take turns defining "generation gap."

Frank: "It's the result of different environments and different interests."

Kit: "It's obvious our parents have had different experience. What's important is how they relate it to their children."

Greg: "It's a lack of concern on both sides for the other group's interests and ideas."

Sharlene: "It has nothing to do with age. You can have a gap with someone fifteen as well as forty. It's not sharing values."

Greg: "It's because everything's changing so much nowadays."

Miriam: "But change is good. It's that somewhere between the desire for change and the fear of it has got to be the right answer. Like this morning I heard something on the air about new electric cars, and I thought, I don't want my kids running around in electric cars—I like good old gas cars. That's a little thing by itself, but it shows people are creatures of habit. They're afraid of what they don't understand. That's why they don't want their children doing new things, trying new ideas."

Jack: "I'm against this thirty-is-the-line idea. I know people above thirty who are what everybody says youth is: I think the term generation gap *clouds* communication."

"You think it's a made-up term with no validity?" I asked.

Frank answered, instead. "I do. I think the radical kids developed the term as a tool for their own purposes—because they don't agree with adults and/or the adults don't agree with them."

Donald Reeves wanted to have his say. Donald is General Organization President at the High School of Music and Art, in New York City, as well as chairman of the student branch of the Student-Parent Faculty Committee. He's 16. "When you say generation gap, you mean a barrier, but that doesn't necessarily mean a conflict. For instance, it can be a barrier of time. Like, take a simple thing—if we went on a date forty years ago, we'd have to be in at nine. Today parents have to get used to our coming in at one."

Karen: "Teens are always trying to use big words like generation gap and make a big deal out of things. I don't get it. My parents and I get along well. Both sides have to recognize the other's interests and value them, even though they might not agree with these different values." Karen speaks with passion, her cheeks reddening. She is a Student Council officer, on the newspaper of Bethlehem (Pennsylvania) Catholic High School, and president of the Senior Senate. She is wearing her Girl Scout uniform and her achievement badges.

Kit: "Can I ask you a question? What would happen, let's say, if you were *not* what you are—a Girl Scout—but became very radical, very much involved, with, let's say, the left wing in your town? And then you tried to explain your position rationally to your parents. Would your parents react rationally then? I think that's the *real* question. The *real* generation gap comes up—I hate the term, it's such a cliché, but it's so good!—when a child does *not* have the same values as his parents and is acting out his life completely different from them. Then either the kid gets obnoxious about it or vice versa."

Karen: "Well, my father and I disagree. He's on the school board, and lots of times when he starts talking politics, especially during the Presidential campaign, we don't see eye to eye. But he usually ends up saying, 'Well, you have your views, and I have mine.' He's great that way."

Kit was not satisfied. "But if you threatened his values with your actions?"

Karen: "Threatened?" Her blue eyes look startled. She is not used to the sophisticated dialogue that comes naturally to a boy attending Middlesex School, in Concord, Massachusetts.

Kit: "I mean, if you acted out what you believe in, if you became involved in a sit-in—"

"It would depend what I was sitting-in for," Karen said quickly.

"For a black-studies program, let's say."

Karen: "Oh, he'd agree with that. But he wouldn't if I were sitting-in for—for boys in the dorms, or something like that."

There was a small explosion of laughter, really to break the tension growing between Karen and Kit. Then Paula spoke up. Paula Terese Trzepacz goes to Pittsfield (Massachusetts) High School. At 16, she is a fragile beauty, with a fine throaty voice and an unruffled manner. She's a good musician (piano, trumpet, and guitar), likes to go "antiquing and mushrooming," is a joiner—everything from Camp Fire Girls to Prom Committee to Christian Doctrine.

"I think that what most of this boils down to," Paula said, "is our parents' fear of progress and fear of their children. The gap gets wider depending on the levels of maturity involved—yours and your parents'. Maturity doesn't come with age. It comes with experience."

There was a round of agreement.

9. Which person most accurately defines the gap between parents and their children?
10. How is it possible for young people to develop different values from the parents who raise them?

Farewell

Written by a grade 12 student from Regina who committed suicide a few weeks later.

He always wanted to explain things.
But no one cared so he drew.
Sometimes he would draw and it wasn't anything.
He wanted to carve it in stone or write it in the sky.
He would be out on the grass and look up in the sky.
And it would be only him and the sky and things inside him
    that needed saying.
And it was after that he drew the picture.
It was a beautiful picture. He kept it under his pillow and
    would let no one see it.
And he would look at it every night and think about it.
And when it was dark, and his eyes were closed, he could
    still see it.
And it was all of him.
And he loved it.
When he started school he brought it with him.
Not to show anyone, but just to have it with him like a friend.
It was funny about school.
He sat at a square brown desk like all the other desks.
In a square brown room like all the other rooms.
And it was tight and close.
And stiff.
He hated to hold the pencil and chalk,
With his arm stiff and his feet flat on the floor.
Stiff.
With the teacher watching and watching.
The teacher came and spoke to him.
She told him to wear a tie like all the other boys.
He said he didn't like them.
And she said it didn't matter!

After that they drew.
And he drew all yellow and it was the way he felt about
  morning.
And it was beautiful.
The teacher came and smiled at him.
'What's this?' she said. 'Why didn't you draw something like
  Ken's drawing?
Isn't it beautiful?'
After that his mother bought him a tie.
And he always drew airplanes and rocket ships like every-
  one else.
And he threw the old picture away.
And when he lay alone looking at the sky, it was big and
  blue and all of everything.
But he wasn't anymore.
He was square inside
And brown.
And his hands were stiff.
And he was like everyone else.
And the things inside him that needed saying didn't need
  it anymore.
It was crushed.
Stiff.
Like everything else.

I had to grow old to learn what I wanted to know,
and I should need to be young to say well what
I know.

                    Joseph Joubert (1842)

Between Parents And Teenagers

by H. Ginott

Many teen-agers have an inner radar that detects what irritates their parents. If we value neatness our teenager will be sloppy, his room messy, his clothes repulsive, and his hair unkempt and long. If we insist on good manners, he will interrupt conversations, use profanity, and belch in company. If we enjoy language that has grace and nuance, he will speak slang. If we treasure peace, he will quarrel with our neighbors, tease their dogs, and bully their children. If we like good literature, he will fill our home with comic books. If we stress physical vigor, he will refuse to exercise. If we are concerned about health, he will wear summer clothes in freezing weather.

Bewildered, parents respond with a predictable sequence of desperate measures. First, we get tough. When this fails, we switch to kindness. When no results follow, we try reasoning. When gentle persuasion falls on deaf ears, we resort to ridicule and rebuke. Then we return to threats and punishment. This is the method of operation of a mutual frustration society.

What can parents do to stay sane and to survive with honor? A famous oriental proverb advises relaxation in face of the inevitable.

Teen-agers rebel in a thousand ways. Our response must differentiate between tolerance and sanction, between acceptance and approval. We tolerate much but sanction little. A parent can tolerate unlikable behavior without sanctioning it.

One father, irritated by his son's long hair, said: "I'm sorry, Son. It's your hair, but it's my guts. I can stand it after breakfast, but not before it. So, please have breakfast in your room."

This response was helpful. Father demonstrated respect for his own feelings. The son was left free to continue with his unpleasant but harmless revolt. Had father sanctioned the hairdo, he would have destroyed its value as a symbol of autonomy and rebellion. More obnoxious behavior might have been substituted by the young rebel.

Wise parents know that fighting a teen-ager, like fighting a riptide, is inviting doom. When caught in a cross-current expert swimmers stop struggling. They know that they cannot fight their way to shore. They float and let the tide carry them, until they find a firm footing. Likewise, parents of teen-agers must flow with life, alert to opportunities for safe contact.

11. Would teenagers act the way they do if parents simply ignored them?
12. Why should the parent adapt to the teenager and not vice versa?

Why They Leave Home

by Rev. Larry Beggs
Rev. Beggs is the founder of a halfway house for runaways.

Few runaways plan their leaving ahead of time. It is an impulsive act but it is also a purposeful action. Running away communicates the seriousness of the adolescent's feeling. It shows his desperation. It shows that there is stress and conflict and his perceived inability to resolve the conflict within the family situation, or that the conditions are not yet ready to allow a resolution. One of the conditions which makes the situation impossible to resolve, is the attitude on the part of the parents that everything is indeed all right. Therefore, there doesn't have to be any talking-out or serious consideration of the feelings of the minor.

Running away, then, is the type of communication that says, "Hey, you've *got* to take my feelings seriously!" Those feelings can be about the issue of long hair, or, more basically, not being allowed to wear it as one chooses. Many adults do not see this as any great thing for young people to be disturbed about. But the young person does.

I think the old story of Samson and Delilah (Judges 16) is a clue perhaps, to how serious this long hair issue is.

Samson, whose strength was supposedly in his hair, was persuaded by Delilah to reveal the secret of his great strength. He said that as a young man he made a Nazarite vow that he would not cut his hair.

So we see that the strength of Samson was not literally in his hair, but in his religious vow not to cut his hair.

As Samson made a religious vow not to cut his hair, the modern young person makes a similar vow. It is the vow to *be himself*. His hair length is part of this vow. Therefore, he looks upon the whole issue of whether he determines the length of his hair as a very serious personal issue. The issue is whether he is to become a *self-directing* individual.

One runaway wrote:

"School also played a great role in my leaving home. In school I was being hassled because the principal thought my hair was too long. This was an extremely asinine role for him to assume, as the role of a teacher in a school is a teacher not a barber. I think I would have learned more if my teachers were more concerned with my schoolwork rather than my hair."

Running away is an effort to communicate the seriousness of feelings involved on the part of the adolescent. Often the young person genuinely believes that he is not being granted enough independent movement or action.

By showing his parents that he can actually survive for a week without much money, that he's not going to be murdered, or that a girl is not necessarily going to lose her virginity and can take care of herself pretty well . . . the runaway challenges his parent's tendency to treat him like a child.

Another thing running away does is challenge the parent's and the school's assumption that everything is indeed all right. Many parents expect their children to be satisfied with material goods. Indeed, the child *has* much more than the parents ever had. Therefore the child should be happy and satisfied with his lot even though his place at home does not allow him any significant decision-making in his life within the family unit. "They give me everything I want except freedom."

13. Do you agree that running away is actually a sign of weakness in character, and not strength?

Thousands of young people walking for charity in "Miles for Millions" march

The Young Re-reviving Ancient Communal Living

by Trent Frayne

Progress, it appears, is not necessarily the act of moving forward.

For example, communes.

Communes are the newest development in youth's progress through the fantastic technology jungle of the 20th century. Communes are the newest product in a society that has been able to pinpoint man's landing on the moon, mass-produce a million cars, and, indeed, virtually eliminate dishpan hands.

But communes are also the wagon trains of a hundred years ago, and in medieval history the towns that grew up in continental Europe after the fall of the Roman Empire were communes.

Still, communes are the newest hip thing, a whole bunch of people with common goals or personalities or attitudes or convictions coming together in small groups to live and love and eat and sleep and work and maybe even take trips together. Without benefit of chaperon.

What they're getting away from, into these communes, is described succinctly by Abbie Hoffman in his new book, *Woodstock Nation*. They're getting away from "a system that channels human beings like so many laboratory rats . . . into a highly mechanized maze of class rankings, degrees, careers, neon supermarkets, military-industrial complexes, suburbs, repressed sexuality, hypocrisy, ulcers and psychoanalysts."

*   *   *

In Canada, there's one more reason: the U.S. military draft. Most of the 55,000 Americans who've come across the border to settle in Ontario in the last three years are draft dodgers who have brought the communal philosophy with them.

But there have been great numbers who have come for those reasons enunciated by Hoffman, too (such as people ineligible for the draft), and even greater numbers who have never seen a Viet Cong in their futures (such as girls.)

And the numbers of Canadians joining communes grows daily.

"Sure, they're coming in all the time," say Jimmy Wilson, a good-looking North Carolinian who was a social worker in New York until he came here with his wife, Patricia, two years ago. "It used to be exclusively U.S., but not any more. In fact, our No. 1 radical is a Canadian from Montreal."

Wilson came to Canada in a yellow truck with all his worldly goods, and eventually opened a small shop on Baldwin St., with meagre capital, selling dresses, candles, leatherwork—in fact, anything he and his wife and a few new acquaintances could manufacture. They called their place the Yellow Ford Truck, and in 14 months it has grown into a loosely joined commune involving about 100 people, nine houses, two stores and two farms.

* * *

Anyone who has read the bestseller *The Naked Ape,* by the zoologist Desmond Morris, will agree that what they're doing is instinctual.

"Hunting apes lived in bands with fixed home bases," Morris wrote.

And again: "Despite all the other advances, the design of our cities and towns is still dominated by our ancient, naked-ape need to divide our groups up into small, discreet, family territories."

And again: "Our behavior is designed to operate in small tribal groups. In such situations every member of the tribe will be known personally to every other member."

And still again: "Cities are very stressful, and in the constant exposure to strangers, anti-touching techniques are developed, i.e., going through crowds without touching, not talking on streetcars, staring at one another."

* * *

Money is the endless obstacle confronting people in communes, even as it assails those they call the straight people. Ideally, most of them would like to operate rural communes, living off the land they cultivate themselves, as thousands of young people are now doing in the warmer areas of the United States.

'Our goal is to move eventually to the country and build a small factory." says Jimmy Wilson of the Yellow Ford Truck, "but continue to operate our stores here, with maybe two people coming down from the country for periods of a few weeks."

His wife, Pat, also a North Carolinian who was a social worker in New York, recalled the other night over a communal dinner that when they, and Cliff and Roz Golas from Boston, started the store in October, 1968, they could barely support themselves.

"Now," she said, smiling, "we can support six people— rent, food and needs—and we have living space and meals for 12 to 15 others in a kind of floating-population way."

They pay $125 a month rent for the store, and $300 a month for a red-brick three-storey house on Dundas St., a couple of blocks from the store.

* * *

Dinner this night was on a come-and-get-it basis. The chef was a grinning young Californian named Sylvester who created an enormous casserole of beef, cheddar cheese, cream sauce, onions and shell noodles. The girls built a savory salad, cooked corn-bread served with Swedish butter, and Sylvester opened several bottles of a chilled Portuguese rosé called Isabella.

Eighteen people sat down to this repast—on the floor, around a wildly cacophonic hi-fi, at the kitchen table, or in easy chairs in a front room.

Prowling the premises and licking cheese from people's fingers were five cats of assorted sizes and sexes rejoicing in such names as Stop Evil Pig, Lucifer, Ra the Sun God, Che and Poohneal.

"Not everybody can adjust to communal life," Jim Wilson noted at one point. "A man who liked his solitude would have a difficult time."

He is 25, wears slightly shaded Peter Fonda-type glasses, is articulate and very composed. He says that most of the people who've come to Canada like it here because, although there's hostility toward the long-haired people, it's not a violent opposition.

"There's sort of a British reserve about them," he observed. "I was shot at once in North Carolina, and of course in the States there are the vigilante groups, the cops and the Ku Klux Klan taking aim on people like us.

"But we're developing a culture we'll fight for if the need comes. The longhairs have been treated like the blacks long enough that they may have to turn to violence themselves. I know that if anybody tried to send me back to the States or tried to shut down the store, I'd fight."

* * *

He was asked about marriage and family-upbringing within communes.

"We don't have all the answers," he said. "We're in a transitional stage. Ideally, the group concept of child-raising would be best for the child—there'd always be a supportive adult around, there'd be more resources for him. The child would always find someone who was feeling affectionate toward him and had the time for him.

"Marriage? Well, what's coming may be serial monogamy. Marriage should only be forever when it works. Otherwise, it could be two weeks or two months or two years."

In this, not much has changed. One difference is that with the straight people there's all that alimony.

14a What values of the "straight" society have the communes retained?
  b. What values have they rejected?
15. Can communes be successful in the twentieth century?

I do want to make it crystal clear that the young people in our country are dedicated and loyal and motivated to improve our society and the government. The kids who go off the reservation in our government are a handful. I bet you couldn't name ten of them.

Nicholas Oganovic, executive director,
U.S. Civil Service Commission

I've Had It Up To Here With The Youth Cult

by Oliver Clausen

But the sad thing is that they (the young) are generally so humorless. The recollection that sticks in my mind, from violent demonstrations I have seen from Berlin to Montreal, is the intensity of pure hatred on those young faces. It bespeaks arrogance and intolerance, total refusal to listen or understand.

A pity, the humorlessness, for there is much in the fantasy world of the young to wax humorous about:

• They pay obeisance to self-indulgence, from sex to drugs to just doing your own thing. Yet their heroes tend to be puritanical revolutionary authoritarians, and indeed total discipline and Spartanism have been preconditions of revolution. Little wonder that to their idols they are but petty bourgeois anarchists.

• They rant, in Canada, against the mythical "American empire" and all its works. Yet their causes and slogans are American—what the New Democratic Party's Charles Taylor calls "colonization of the mind."

• They demand instant Utopia, as children will. But if any such state could ever be brought about, what on earth would they find to rebel against—for rebel, it seems now accepted, the young must?

• Again on the subject of fixation on the United States, that is where around the world they look for the needed diabolism (the Nazis also had the Jews) and where the Movement (oh, another stock Nazi designation at the moment has gone to its greatest extremes. Yet the latter is because the United States is the *least* oppressive of societies, even in wartime tolerating the waving of a terrorist enemy's flag. Now for a little anti-government demonstrating in Havana or Moscow or, say, by Tibetans in Peking . . .

But it's not really to be made fun of, this. It may be hard to take even the utterly alienated young very seriously *in themselves*. Their overpowering herd instinct, their eagerness to submerge individual dignity in the like-minded, like-appearing mob, and in orgasms of noise that preclude individual thought, do raise apprehension about what they can be *made* to do.

Bruno Bettelheim, the Austrian-born psychologist who thinks New Leftists and the rest are emotionally sick, has some thoughts about how easily the young are shaped like putty by society's attitudes:

"The original hippies—very sick people, very sweet people —wanted to be nothing but left alone. If they had been, most of them would have found their way back sooner or later. By becoming glorified in the public eye, being weak to begin with, they were sucked into a life that became utterly destructive to them."

That, surely, is a large part of it: the responsibility of adult society as a whole for the youth cult which has created what Aldridge calls the royal family of adolescence. It is probably, at least in North America, of graver concern than any prospective deliberate manipulation of youth for political purposes. Some of the young may, fantasy-like, praise alien tyrants, which Dr. Bettelheim explains with the observation that "unconsciously their commitment to Mao and leaders like him suggests their desperate need for controls from outside, since without them they cannot bring order to their own inner chaos." Therefore, and because if Mao is my father's enemy he's my ally. But it is the myopic attitude of society right here, rather than any distant Maoist myth, that is responsible for the youth cult phenomenon.

It is easy enough to pinpoint specific examples of adults being subjugated by the cult. There is the prurient voyeurism about adolescent sex on stage and screen, the pandering in the media to juvenile demands and prejudices, . . . the adoption by grownups of youthful fads in hirsuteness and garb—as if pathetically trying to become kids again.

I have not encountered this to anything like the same extent in Europe. One reason may be that we are an intrinsically childish people, whether or not groping for some lost innocence that Europeans have long since given up hope of recovering. What can be more childish than a Shriners' convention or indeed almost any

North American political or other rally? Little wonder, bearing such things in mind, that North Americans find it peculiarly tempting to indulge the cult of those who really *are* young, even if they earn nothing but contempt in return.

Again harking back to the Thirties—which I cannot resist doing because I grew up under what started as a youth cult Movement then—I see a special danger inherent in this. North America's young, always the most spoiled of all, have been brought up in expectation of getting everything almost at once, simply for the asking (those who have not, the poor in the ghettos, have lately developed a compensating propensity for *taking*). They may not realize that essentially only superficial things are involved in adults' neurotic hankering to get a piece of the cult action.

Where do they turn their tribal rage when, as must happen, they find that there are things they just cannot have? Or when adult society stops playing indulgent games with them and they see that this is all it has been?

That, too, has to happen. Among other things, the young are so boring.

16. In an entirely honest evaluation of today's young people, which of the following phrases (adapted from the article) are accurate, at least in part?
    a) humorless
    b) arrogant and intolerant
    c) alienated
    d) spoiled
    e) desperately wanting controls
    f) herd-like
    g) boring

The management of Fairbank Lumber Co. wish to express sincere thanks to the Firemen and Police whose efforts prevented major damage to our premises as a result of the disastrous fire in an adjoining lumber yard. Special thanks also to those citizens including teenagers, for their help in moving stock to safety and in controlling crowds of spectators who had entered our yard.

THINK

(a) Resolved: That today's young people are no different than young people have ever been.

(b) Resolved: That young people are not activists seeking to change society, but instead are victims of a way of life to which they are simply reacting.

(c) "Young people today have a disgusting unwillingness to discuss anything. They are narrow-minded, stubborn, shockingly uninformed, and mob-oriented." To what extent are these accusations true?

(d) Young people have been accused of being all style and no substance. What does this mean? Is it true?

(e) To what extent is the generation gap the fault of modern-day mass communication?

(f) "What these kids need is a darn good depression. They've just got too much money, and that's all that's wrong with them." (grandfather of nine young people) Can there be a generation gap in a society where there is little money?

(g) In your opinion, are rules good for teenagers?
What rules do you think should be imposed on dating? on entertaining at home? on dress? on spending money?

(h) Are today's teenagers better equipped to make decisions for themselves than their parents were?

(i) Why has our society always given near-heroic status to those teenagers in literature who exhibit initiative, independence, and even rebelliousness?

> e.g. David Copperfield
> Huck Finn and Tom Sawyer
> Holden Caulfield

9. THE LAW IN A DEMOCRACY

1. The man talking to the girl in the picture is a policeman working undercover. So are the two men on the porch stoop behind him. Do you agree that agents of the law should actively seek out potential lawbreakers in this way?

Chasing The Weed

by Reginald Whittaker

John Lennon once described cannabis as a "harmless giggle," but when he was arrested and convicted of possession it turned out to be neither harmless nor a giggle. Lennon happens to be one of the more prominent victims of the laws against cannabis, but there are thousands less well known all over Canada, the United States and Britain who have found out just what the state will do to 'protect' people from themselves.

André Grandbois was twenty-four years old, with a grade-five education, and homeless in Montreal. During the spring and summer of 1968 two undercover RCMP agents, posing as hippies, met Grandbois. Grandbois sold a cube of hashish to one of these agents for seven dollars at the latter's request. He was arrested and sentenced to two years in St. Vincent de Paul penitentiary. In sentencing Grandbois the judge made it very clear just what real issues were at stake.

"The hippies never cease to affirm that they do not disturb anyone, that they lead a peaceful existence, that each individual has the right to live his life as he wishes. The Court does not share in this opinion . . . because any life within a society requires an active and constructive participation on the part of the individuals the society is composed of.

At a time when, in Canada and more than ever in Quebec, everyone is convinced that more and more advanced education is required for facing life and when enormous amounts of money are invested on this basis, these young hippies decide to do nothing, permit themselves to criticize everything, live in unhealthy environments, look for euphoria through the absorption of narcotics, traffic in narcotics and affirm that consuming marijuana or hashish is not unhealthy *per se* and that they are free to dispose of their life and their persons as they see fit.

The Court can only condemn the deplorable way of life which these young people have adopted."

2. Resolved: That because André Grandbois is a member of society, he is, therefore, required to participate actively and constructively in that society.
3. Is the purpose of the law:
   (a) to protect society?
   (b) to protect the rights of the individual?
   (c) to punish law-breakers?
   (d) to prevent crime?

On Liberty (1895)

by John Stuart Mill

The object of this Essay is to assert one very simple principle, as entitled to govern absolutely the dealings of society with the individual in the way of compulsion and control, whether the means used be physical force in the form of legal penalties, or the moral coercion of public opinion. That principle is, that the sole end for which mankind are warranted, individually or collectively, in interfering with the liberty of action of any of their number, is self-protection. That the only purpose for which power can be rightfully exercised over any member of a civilized community, against his will, is to prevent harm to others. His own good, either physical or moral, is not a sufficient warrant. He cannot rightfully be compelled to do or forbear because it will be better for him to do so, because it will make him happier, because, in the opinions of others, to do so would be wise, or even right. These are good reasons for remonstrating with him, or reasoning with him, or persuading him, or entreating him, but not for compelling him, or visiting him with any evil in case he do otherwise. To justify that, the conduct from which it is desired to deter him, must be calculated to produce evil to some one else. The only part of the conduct of any one, for which he is amenable to society, is that which concerns others. In the part which merely concerns himself, his independence is, of right, absolute. Over himself, over his own body and mind, the individual is sovereign.

4a. Does Mill's premise contradict the argument of the judge in *Chasing The Weed?*
  b. By Mill's principles, did the RCMP violate individual liberty in the Grandbois case?

Judge Bans Child Auction

RECIFE, Brazil—(UPI)—

A judge has banned the main attraction at nearby Cupira's rural fair—the sale of a four-year-old child who had been scheduled to be auctioned with the bulls and boars tomorrow.

Yesterday's ban followed an announcement by Lourival José Luna and his wife, Maria, that they would auction their son Lamartine to fulfill a religious pledge to St. Joseph.

Judge Antonio Barrios Silva said the sale violated Brazil's anti-slavery laws and told the Cupira police chief Lt. José Capitulino Andrade, to prevent it.

Mr. Luna had vowed in prayers to St. Joseph to sell Lamartine, youngest of his seven children, if he was cured of a skin disease afflicting him since infancy. He promised to donate the proceeds of the sale to the Church.

The Majesty Of The Law

Without a system of law, and respect for that system of law, civilization, as we know it, would cease to exist. The very basis of interaction among individuals depends upon belief in and deference toward a body of accepted principles that are apart from, and yet a part of, those individuals.

Think of the transactions of an average individual in an average day. Before beginning even the daily activities of his life, he cleans himself, eats, and dresses. All the amenities he uses have been made safe by regulation; so has his food and his clothing. And this factor of safety and function applies to the rest of his day. Everything he does is made possible by law.

The most profound argument in favor of a thorough legal system is any situation that develops anarchy. Witness the terror bombings and kidnappings of the FLQ in Quebec, the race riots of the 1960's in the United States, the student riots in France, the hunger riots in India. When situations like these arise, there is no law save that of survival-of-the-fittest. There is no safety, no guarantee of property, no assurance of redress, no purpose, no cooperation — no life! Only with the restoration of order by means of a force acting within the law, that is, in the interests of the majority, does a civilized mode of living return.

Law is the only alternative to anarchy. It must be held in majesty and awe.

5. Does "respect for the law" mean "respect for authority"?
6a. What pleasant aspects of your own life are made possible by law?
 b. Is any part of your pattern of daily living made unpleasant by the law?
7. "The will of the majority": Who constitutes the majority?

PROCLAMATION.

BY His Excellency SIR FRANCIS BOND HEAD, Baronet, Lieutenant Governor of Upper Canada, &c. &c.

To the Queen's Faithful Subjects in Upper Canada.

In a time of profound peace, while every one was quietly following his occupations, feeling secure under the protection of our Laws, a band of Rebels, instigated by a few malignant and disloyal men, has had the wickedness and audacity to assemble with Arms, and to attack and Murder the Queen's Subjects on the Highway—to Burn and Destroy their Property—to Rob the Public Mails—and to threaten to Plunder the Banks—and to Fire the City of Toronto.

Brave and Loyal People of Upper Canada, we have been long suffering from the acts and endeavours of concealed Traitors, but this is the first time that Rebellion has dared to shew itself openly in the land, in the absence of invasion by any Foreign Enemy.

Let every man do his duty now, and it will be the last time that we or our children shall see our lives or properties endangered, or the Authority of our Gracious Queen insulted by such treacherous and ungrateful men. MILITIA-MEN OF UPPER CANADA, no Country has ever shewn a finer example of Loyalty and Spirit than YOU have given upon this sudden call of Duty. Young and old of all ranks, are flocking to the Standard of their Country. What has taken place will enable our Queen to know Her Friends from Her Enemies—a public enemy is never so dangerous as a concealed Traitor—and now my friends let us complete well what is begun—let us not return to our rest till Treason and Traitors are revealed to the light of day, and rendered harmless throughout the land.

Be vigilant, patient and active—leave punishment to the Laws—our first object is, to arrest and secure all those who have been guilty of Rebellion, Murder and Robbery.—And to aid us in this, a Reward is hereby offered of

One Thousand Pounds,

to any one who will apprehend, and deliver up to Justice, WILLIAM LYON MACKENZE; and FIVE HUNDRED POUNDS to any one who will apprehend, and deliver up to Justice, DAVID GIBSON—or SAMUEL LOUNT—or JESSE LLOYD—or SILAS FLETCHER—and the same reward and a free pardon will be given to any of their accomplices who will render this public service, except he or they shall have committed, in his own person, the crime of Murder or Arson.

And all, but the Leaders above-named, who have been seduced to join in this unnatural Rebellion, are hereby called to return to their duty to their Sovereign—to obey the Laws—and to live henceforward as good and faithful Subjects—and they will find the Government of their Queen as indulgent as it is just.

GOD SAVE THE QUEEN.

Monday, 3 o'clock, P. M.
7th Dec.

☞ The Party of Rebels, under their Chief Leaders, is wholly dispersed, and flying before the Loyal Militia. The only thing that remains to be done, is to find them, and arrest them.

Is Our System Weakening?

The legal systems of democratic countries are a part of the people's way of life. Certain philosophic principles are woven into the very fabric of the society. The right of trial by one's peers, for example, is a privilege that the citizens of a democratic country take as a matter of course. So is the principle that one is entitled to defend himself in a court of law, or that one is presumed innocent until proven guilty. These principles and others like them are not just a part of the system—they *are* the system.

So ingrained is the acceptance of the system that only by conquest, it is generally believed, can it be overthrown. But the complexities of twentieth century life, and a general eroding of faith in traditional values, are exposing what may be inherent weaknesses.

Bobby Seale, leader of the Black Panthers, a militant group that first gained national recognition at the famous 1968 Democratic Convention in Chicago managed to turn his trial for "conspiracy to riot," into a complete farce. Seale, contending that his trial was invalid, refused to abide by the time-honored rules, and made so many noisy disruptions that he was eventually gagged and manacled to a chair. In other words, the defendant in essence, was not permitted to participate in his own trial. This leads to a rather serious question: "If a man rejects a legal system, and is still tried by the system, is the system, therefore, undemocratic?"

Countries like South Africa, where apartheid policies preclude the giving of all rights to black people, are practising an immoral system. One might well ask, "Is the legal system of a country like South Africa immoral because its policies are immoral? Does morality precede legality?"

Another problem seems to have surfaced since the 1960's. Whereas the glory of western society's legal system is inherent in such landmarks as the Magna Carta or the Bill Of Rights which guarantee individual freedom, the actual base and practice of the law seems, more and more, to be *property*. Another question to ponder: "Is a legal system designed only for those who have vested interests?" And then: "What have the poor to gain from obeying the law?"

Jurists have asked these questions before and have found academic answers. But today these questions are being asked by black people in Louisiana, by Indians in western Canada, and by the poor everywhere. Academic answers may no longer suffice.

*   *   *

9. Where do *you* stand on the questions posed by this article?

. . . it is the poor who suffer most from society masked in the trappings of the law.

John Turner,
Canadian Minister of Justice

Spent 34 Years In Jail For $5 Candy Theft, He Asks Compensation

WASHINGTON, (AP)— Stephen Dennison, 60, appealed today to the U.S. Supreme Court for $115,000 for the 34 years he spent in prison for stealing $5 worth of chocolate bars and marshmallows.

Through lawyers, the unemployed Glens Falls, N.Y., janitor said the money, once awarded him by a claims court, would be partial compensation for "the lifetime he could never enjoy."

The award was set aside by New York appeals courts on the grounds that Dennison, classified by reformatory officials as a "low-grade moron," could not hold the state liable even if state doctors were wrong in ruling him mentally defective.

As a boy of 16, Dennison was arrested for stealing the candy from a roadside stand in his hometown, Salem, N.Y. He was given a suspended sentence and placed on probation. When he did not report monthly to a minister, he was sent to the Elmira reformatory.

There officials decided he was mentally deficient. He was transferred to an institution for male defective delinquents at Naponach, N.Y., and later to the Dannemora State Hospital.

In 1960, after 34 years in state institutions, he was released through the efforts of a brother, George, who was convinced he was sane.

The biggest sentence Dennison could have received for the $5 theft was 10 years. His lawyers contend the additional 24 years were imposed unconstitutionally, that Dennison should have been given a jury trial where he could have fought the doctors' conclusions.

They added: "The money that would be awarded to Dennison is not a fine or a penalty imposed upon the people of New York—it is merely a small measure of compensation to him for the loss that he sustained."

Millionaire Tried In Closed Court

MILTON, (Staff)—Halton County Crown Attorney Douglas Latimer has admitted that a charge of threatening against a prominent Oakville millionaire was tried in Family Court last week to avoid publicity.

Mr. Latimer said it was felt that "in the best interests of the persons involved it would be better if the charge was heard in Family Court."

At the closed court appearance Wednesday, George Clinton Jones Duke, the 65-year-old president of Duke Lawn Equipment Ltd., admitted he used a .38-calibre revolver to threaten the life of Mrs. Elizabeth Citron of Waterdown.

Mr. Duke, who weighs 200 pounds and is six foot three inches tall, was ordered by Judge Kenneth Langdon to post a $2,000 bond to keep the peace for a year and to stay away from Mrs. Citron.

His permit to carry a revolver for his own protection was revoked.

The incident occurred when Mr. Duke went to Mrs. Citron's home and demanded to know where his wife was. Mrs. Citron and Mrs. Duke are friends.

Mrs. Citron said that when she told Mr. Duke she didn't know where his wife was he threatened to kill her.

A private complaint was sworn out by Mrs. Citron before Justice of the Peace William Daniels.

"In this county we feel that in these cases involving families the best interests of all concerned and the best interests of justice are served if the complaint is heard in Family Court," Mr. Latimer said.

"The matter was discussed very thoroughly by myself, the judge and the defence counsel.

"As far as I am aware Mrs. Citron was very satisfied with the handling of the case and its outcome."

9. Aside from the overwhelming obvious fact of money, for what other reasons might a wealthier person fare better in court than a poor person?

French writer and politician Alexis de Tocqueville, said in his analysis of American democracy (1833) that America was the freest and, at the same time, the most despotic nation on Earth. Because the citizen chooses his own government, he is, by definition, free. Yet, on the other hand, this same government acts as the oppressive instrument of the majority. Through the minute regulation of the social and private life of the individual in the interests of equality, de Tocqueville noted, all local and individual differences are eventually eradicated.

---

10. Should a man who owns his own establishment be allowed to refuse service to a person of another race if he wishes?

A man should *be* upright, not be *kept* upright.
Marcus Aurelius

The Future for the Law

excerpts from a speech made by Canadian Minister of Justice John Turner

It has been said that the greatest achievement of the 60's is that we survived them . . . .

We are witnessing today what has been called a "crisis of legitimacy," or as some would have it, a "crisis of authority."

All our institutions — the state, the university, the family, and, of particular concern to us, the law — are being challenged.

The challenge reaches not only the laws but those who make the laws. It strikes at the very legitimacy of the legal order itself. In a revolutionary climate, the law is considered the antithesis of revolution.

In a mood of alienation, the law is regarded as a false consciousness. In an impatient world, the law is perceived as the curator of reaction.

I believe, however, that the law is still relevant, and can be made more relevant in contemporary terms; that authority and freedom are not contradictory but complementary; that they need not be opposed but juxtaposed; that law is not the enemy of revolution, but that "revolution" can be made possible through law.

Indeed, in an age of confrontation our social problems become our legal problems. The problems of the 60s are now the legal challenges of the 70s. Society itself has become the lawyer's client, and society will hold the law to account.

The faith that must move us, then, is the creative and even revolutionary role that law can play in the building and restructuring of a new society. . . .

First, we must redress the imbalance in the relationship between the individual and the state. The bigness and remoteness of government must not be allowed further to obscure or dwarf individual rights. . . .

Secondly, Canada needs a more contemporary criminal law—credible, enforceable, flexible and compassionate.

If we are to have a just society, we must begin with just laws; and nowhere is this more important than in the realm of criminal law; for it is here that the most fundamental values of life, liberty, property and dignity are to be protected and sanctioned, and it is here that the measure of our commitment to these values will be tested. . . .

We must disabuse ourselves of the myth that the criminal law sanction falls with equal impact on all segments of society. Indeed, it may well be—as some studies have pointed out—that our laws, such as vagrancy and public drunkenness, and our courts that administer them, have made it virtually a crime to be poor in public. And so it is that the *condition* of poverty may become the rationale for criminalization. . . .

Third, we must promote equality of access and equality of treatment before the law for rich and poor, young and old, alike.

The adversary process before the courts must become a more meaningful, and less of a mythical, operation, particularly as it relates to the young, the dispossessed, the disenchanted, and the urban poor. . . .

We will have to harness technology in the service of the law rather than leave law at the mercy of technology.

It will be necessary, then, to explore initiatives in the whole area of environmental control and probe the questions of interactive dynamics between science, technology and the law. For while technology races, the law lags; and once again the scientists are beating the lawyers.

Pollution is a good example of this. We are choking our environment and being choked in return. . . .

For if the war on pollution is to be won—indeed, if it is to be fought at all—a comprehensive national and international legal regime will have to be developed and applied.

Also, if the war on pollution is to be won we must abandon our "vandal ideology" which has permitted us to ravage our environment.

Ecology is the relationship between man and his environment; and law is the ordering of the relationships between man and his environment—the organizing principle of society.

11. "Authority and freedom are not contradictory but complementary." Right?
12. Do Mr. Turner's proposals for the Canadian system imply that the system has been wrong all along, or that the needed changes have just developed in the twentieth century?

THINK

(a) Do you know of anything that is illegal but not immoral?
(b) What is the difference between civil rights and civil liberties?
(c) A supreme court justice in the United States has said that his country is becoming a quick-draw society in which righteous people will arm themselves just as in frontier days. Should people who obey the law have the right to protect themselves, in any way they choose, from people who do not?
(d) "If our democracy cannot handle a few extremists, it's not very real." (from *Black Phoenix,* CBC TV Drama) Does our society tolerate extremism?
(e) A prominent North American doctor once told a group of lawyers that he would never testify, under any circumstances, against another doctor. The lawyers were shocked. Why were the lawyers so upset? On what reasoning would the doctor base his assertion?
(f) To what extent are our laws based on custom?
(g) Resolved: That law is a thing which can accomplish goals that people themselves are incapable of achieving.
(h) Resolved: That "He who tries to determine everything by law will foment crime rather than lessen it."
(i) Try to make a list of the ways in which the state interfered with the daily lives of people in the eighteenth century. Compare it with a list from the twentieth century.

10. SCHOOL IS....

Your Attention Please! This Is The Office.

Ignore the bell you just heard. The fire bell is dong dong dong; the dismissal bell is ding ding. . . .
Period two will come after period seven today. . . .
The game today begins at 2:30. Get out and cheer for our team. Students will be dismissed at 3:10. . . .
Would the owner of the green MG parked in the driveway please call his insurance company. . . .
The clocks are not working today. Twenty to five is actually ten after nine. . . .
There will be no announcements today. . . .

"People who tell you that you need all the education you can get hold of are not trying to cajole you into continuing at school: they are stating an undeniable fact. We are living in a time when you need to know about things that were not even in the dictionary when your father was young. And we are entering upon an age when what we learn this year and next will be all too little to keep our heads above water. By all means reach out your hands for all the learning you can grasp, and give your minds to mastering it."

Chief General Manager
Royal Bank of Canada

Stay In School — The Magnificent Obsession

excerpts from a speech by Walter Pitman, member of Parliament and former teacher.

"It is my observation that we have become obsessed with formal education, i.e. schooling. This is understandable as we have passed through a decade during which our worship of the formal education process has been total. We have been led to believe that formal education will civilize our youth, and make them employable citizens. Indeed, this concept has led us to generalize that education is the last hope of mankind and is the only path we can hope to tread towards a world in which poverty, unemployment and sickness are to be banished.

We are realizing now that simply increasing access has not meant automatic equality of educational opportunity. The reason has been quite simple. Children from culturally deprived, economically depressed homes do not succeed in an atmosphere and structure previously prepared for children of middle and higher incomes. They are "turned off" by the values, teaching methods, the teacher and administration attitudes which confront them.

Real equality of education would demand a reaching out to the poor family, the encouragement of community programs, to bring home and school together, even to the extent of parent participation in the activities of the school.

I have belaboured the problem of securing real equality of educational opportunity because it relates very closely to my next point, that we should search out ways of getting kids out of school, rather than continue the present policy of institutionalizing young people by legislation to the age of 16, and by social pressure to the age of 21 or 22. Once we end the possibility that young people will be pushed out of school because they are poor or culturally deprived, emotionally disturbed or ethnically oriented, then we can discuss rationally the proposition that to many young people, school is not the best place for them to learn from the age of 16 to 22.

We have heard a great deal about educational reform, but there is really more concern with a re-arrangement of curriculum "boxes," and changes in teaching method and administrative procedure. In a decade of profound change, is this an adequate reaction on the part of the formal education system? Are we really on a rational course in a century promising an urbanized, technological society, with the hope of greater leisure, and greater opportunities for a higher quality of life for all?

I think most of the unrest of young people today is centred on the desire to live creatively. They resent the continuous "hot-house" of the school environment. They want some experience "out there." They want to test their mental muscles, they want to become involved in real causes. Their idealism is monumental, and in an age of participation, they want to get in on the action. Yet they must stay in school, stay in University, stay in the C.A.A.T., or no job, no future.

As well, we are carrying on quite suspect practices in the name of education. We try to teach history, the story of man's greed and ambition, to children who scarcely have any sense of time, to say little of any experience with their fellows. Now we are dropping subjects like psychology, sociology, anthropology, economics, down into the secondary school. Once again, with no maturity, with no background of experience, so much of this "learning" is of limited long-term value.

Is it any wonder that many young people feel that they are being kept in school, because we, as adults, do not have the wit to end methods of tapping their energy, imagination and idealism. We can best keep them off the labour market, we can best keep them "out of our hair."

And rightly so, as long as the educational system is looked upon in isolation to the total society. But how much more civilized, how much more educationally rational, that many young people should leave some time in secondary school, be given training in short-term skills and be encouraged to return when they have both intellectual and emotional learning readiness.

And this is where the businessman comes into the picture. I can see many opportunities in the public sector, jobs in schools, as teacher aides and assistants, in needed nursery schools, in facilities for aged, in institutions for emotionally disturbed, in penal institutions, to say nothing of the great causes to end pollution, build low cost housing and so on. We can break down many professional tasks, in health services and engineering. Do we have any right to expect that business and industry could organize itself to accept young people with a particular short-term skill, for a limited period of time?

I think that there is probably no more inefficient form of activity than adolescent education. Consider a cost-benefit study for many young people in Grade 11. How much is really learned, at what public expense? And would the subject-matter, or better, some more relevant material, be learned in a fraction of the time and at a fraction of the expense, to the benefit of all, a few years later? This is certainly the view of the adult educationalist, and there is much to suggest he is dead right.

1. What are the basic problems in the education system as Mr. Pitman sees them?
2. Are there flaws in his proposal that adolescents work for a while and then return to school when they are more mature?
3. Would *you* leave school now if you were allowed to do so? Would you like to leave now, knowing that in two years you would be returning?
4. Why is education such a popular target for criticism and suggested changes?

> I have never let my schoolin' interfere with my
> education.
>
> Mark Twain

What Is Education For?

from Living And Learning

The heart of the problem of providing a general education in a democratic society is to ensure the continuance of
the liberal and human tradition.

This is far more basic to our society than the worship of
intellectual pursuits and scientific endeavors for their own
sake. It must be recognized that the nourishment of such a
precious commodity as freedom requires that the educational
process, if it is not to fall short of the ideal, include at each
level of growth and development some continuing experience
in making value judgments. Whitehead, the great British
philosopher, has said that all students must have before them
the "habitual vision of greatness." Unless they feel the import
of the ideas and aspirations which have been a deep and
moving force in the lives of great men, students run the risk
of inspirational blindness.

What is new, exciting, and thought-provoking in our era
is that what was once the privilege of an elite has now become the right of a multitude. How to provide learning experience aiming at a thousand different destinies and at the
same time to educate toward a common heritage and common citizenship, is the basic challenge to our society. Thus

democracy must not only provide an opportunity for the able; it must seek to provide betterment for the less endowed, both by immediate improvement which can be gained in a generation, and by the slow surge of advancement which works through several generations. The gifted and talented should not be allowed to become undernourished by mediocre aspirations, and the slow learners and handicapped should not be stigmatized as failures. Each human being is deserving of respect, identity, and the right to develop toward the fulfilment of his unique potential. In the democratic society all men are of equal importance, and none is expendable.

In a democratic society, it is not the task of education to stress the thousand influences and labels dividing man from man, but to establish the necessary bonds and common ground between them. The great art of education lies in providing learning experiences which meet the needs of each, and which at the same time foster that feeling of compassion among human beings which is the greatest strength and bulwark of democracy.

Those procedures in an educational system which encircle and differentiate groups of children and adolescents and create chasms between them, can nurture seeds of misunderstanding, discontent, and class distinctions. Even within schools, insurmountable walls and psychological barriers can be built between children of different potentials; this, in actuality, creates schools within schools, divides students from students, and seals them off from one another.

The beacon to guide the truth-seekers of tomorrow is dependent for its fuel upon the freedom exercised by society today. We cannot efford to lose our great and vital heritage through default, ennui, or lack of commitment. A free society cannot be taken for granted, and truth and freedom must be guarded as precious treasures. Each of us has the right to enjoy them. More than that, we have the obligation to protect them, and we each must have the courage to accept and embrace the responsibilities that they hold out to us each day.

5. Precisely what do *you* hope to gain by going to school? How do your objectives relate to the objectives expressed in this passage?
6. The content of this passage has been called an "impossible dream." What is there in it that would cause such a reaction? Do you agree that it is an impossible dream?

In Yamaguchi, Japan, a teacher, Kazuo Tomita, was fired by his school board for discussing the teachings of Mao Tse-Tung with his students and giving them copies of Mao's quotations. The board said he was violating the law by giving education from a "special point of view."

The Way It Spozed To Be

by John Herndon

Nothing had been mentioned in the meeting about a system of classification involving A's and B's, but inquiry around the coffee tables in the teachers' room had informed me that the kids were all rated A (high) to H (low) and placed in classrooms together accordingly. The ratings were made on the basis of IQ tests, standardized achievement tests, and, on occasion, faculty recommendation. Added to this imposing number of groups were a couple of classes which were supposed to be retarded and were naturally taught in the basement. I didn't know this detail until later on in the year, but I mention it now to complete the student body.

It is this kind of classification, based on this kind of testing, which seems to me the perfect example of the kind of thing that continually goes on in a school, and for which there is no reasonable explanation. Talking just to any teacher, as I did that year, you can hear a perfectly plausible lecture to the effect that IQ (or Mental Maturity, as it now goes) tests are not particularly valid under the best of conditions—that is, their validity is only general. You can't say, for example, that a child who scores 120 is any more capable than one who scores 116, 112, or anything above, say, 100. The Achievement Tests, which hope to measure what the child has actually learned in school, rather than what he may be capable of learning, have results equally hazardous of interpretation. If they tend to place a seventh-grade child at grade level 7.6, has that child actually learned more than the 7.1 or 6.9 child, and has he learned less than the 7.9 or the 8.2? Does one take tests well and another badly? Did one spend the sixth grade being drilled on punctuation and another writing science-fiction stories? Does one like to read? Was one ill when map-reading was going on? Did he have ringworm? Was he in Juvenile Hall? The questions are endless and also nonsensical, presenting you with a perfect (William) Jamesian confrontation but not, of course, much good for anything else.

7. What is the purpose of standardized tests?
8. What are the advantages and disadvantages of homogeneous class groupings?

Students don't ask that orders make sense. They give up expecting things to make sense long before they leave elementary school. Things are true because the teacher says they're true. At a very early age we all learn to accept "two truths," as did certain medieval churchmen. Outside of class, things are true to your tongue, your fingers, your stomach, your heart. Inside class, things are true by reason of authority. And that's just fine because you don't care anyway.

from *The Student As Nigger*
by Jerry Farber

My Experience In A Free School

by Dale J————[*aged 16*]

At first I couldn't believe it! There were no desks in rows; no bells rang; nobody *had* to go to class. Although we all lived "in", nobody made us go to bed at a certain time; there was no "lights out".

The strange thing was though, that practically all the students went to class, and very few people stayed up late at night. Only the new people—those who came for their first time—stayed up or skipped class. The new ones always went wild at first, but this never lasted long. The freedom took some getting used to. Our teachers treated us like adults; never did we have to play "stand up", "sit down", "speak out". And although this was very strange at first, we really responded. I don't know of one kid who didn't try his best.

The subjects were the same as regular school, but what a difference in the approach! For example, in botany we had no classes in the spring or fall, but instead we planted two gardens, a vegetable garden and a flower garden. Then in winter we each studied a few particular things about what we had grown. In math the kids built three different kinds of sheds—small ones of course, but usable. They did this instead of studying geometry and statics. They really had a terrific time too, designing everything, drawing the blueprints, figuring out the angles and the foot-pounds of force and all that stuff. As you can probably guess, I didn't take math. I can't stand it! Besides, I can add, subtract, multiply, and divide. That's enough! And because there were no compulsory subjects, I didn't take math.

In spite of all the differences, the teachers were no better than in regular school. Frankly I think my regular school teachers were more interesting as people. But that, I suppose, is just the luck of the draw.

On the whole I think I am a much better person for having gone to the school. I can read and write as well as anyone else my age, and I can *think* better. (That's probably one of the big difference between the free school and regular school —the amount of *thinking*.) I didn't exactly learn any manners, and because no one bugged us about cleanliness, I got downright sloppy at times. And I wouldn't exactly say that the place taught me to be a lady! But then it isn't necessary. I can be clean if I want to. I know how to be a lady if I want to. The most important thing is what happened inside me. Would you believe that I haven't had a fight with anyone— even a quarrel—in over a year! And that includes my mother!

9. In a free school situation, where everyone is treated as an equal, is it likely that the level of behaviour, dress, manners, and morals will sink to the lowest common denominator?

10. Would a free school system such as Dale described, work in a large publicly supported school system?
11. "I would rather see a school produce a happy street cleaner than a neurotic scholar." Should a person always try to better himself?

Discipline In the Seventeenth Century

from Ludus Literarius *by John Brimsley, published in 1612*

In this correction with the rod, special provision must be had for sundry things.

I. That when you are to correct any stubborn or unbroken boy, you may be sure with him to hold him fast; as they are enforced to do who are to shoe or to tame an unbroken colt. To this end appoint three or four of your scholars, whom you know to be honest, and strong enough, or more if need be, to lay hands upon him together, to hold him fast, over some form, so that he cannot stir hand nor foot; or else if no other remedy will serve, to hold him to some post (which is far the safest and free from inconvenience) so as he cannot anyway hurt himself or others, be he never so peevish. Neither that he can have hope by any device or turning, or by his apparel, or any other means to escape. Nor yet that any one be left in his stubbornness to go away murmuring, pouting, or blowing and puffing, until he shew as much submission as any, and that he will lie still of himself without any holding; yet so as ever a wise moderation be kept. Although this must of necessity be looked unto; because besides the evil example to others, there is no hope to do any good to count of with any, till their stomachs be first broken: and then they once thoroughly brought under, you may have great hope to work all good according to their capacity; so that it may be, you have little occasion to correct them after. Moreover, every child suffered in his stubbornness to escape for his struggling, will in a short time come to trouble two or three men to take him up and to correct him without danger of hurting himself, or others.

II. To be wary for smiting them over the backs, in any case, or in such sort as in any way to hurt or endanger them. To the end to prevent all mischiefs, for our own comfort; and to cut off all occasions from quarrelling parents or evil reports of the school. And withal, to avoid for these causes, all smiting them upon the head, with hand, rod or ferula. Also to the end that we may avoid all danger and fear for desperate boys hurting themselves, not to use to threaten them afore, and when they have done any notorious fault, nor to let them know when they shall be beaten; but when they commit a new fault, or that we see the school most full or opportunity most fit, to take them of a sudden.

III. That the master do not in any case abase himself to strive or struggle with any boy to take him up: but to appoint other of the strongest to do it, where such need is, in such sort as was shewed before; and the rather for fear of hurting them in his anger, and for the evils which may come thereof and which some schoolmasters have lamented after.

IV. That the masters and ushers also do by all means avoid all furious anger, threatening, chafing, fretting, reviling: for these things will diminish authority and may do much hurt, and much endanger many ways. And therefore on the contrary, that all their correction be done with authority, and with a wise and sober moderation, in a demonstration of duty to God and love to the children, for their amendment, and the reformation of their evil manners.

Finally, as God hath sanctified the rod and correction, to cure the evils of their conditions, to drive out that folly which is bound up in their hearts, to save their souls from hell, to give them wisdom; so it is to be used as God's instrument to these purposes. To spare them in these cases is to hate them. To love them is to correct them betime. Do it under God, and for Him to these ends and with these cautions, and you shall never hurt them: you have the Lord for your warrant. Correction, in such manner, for stubbornness, negligence and carelessness, is not to be accounted over-great severity, much less cruelty.

12. What is the rationale that supports strong discipline?
13. What would your school be like if every disciplinary restraint were rescinded?
— What would be the immediate reaction?
— What would school be like in a week?
— What would it be like in six months?

It's the kids that have to be educated first; they're apathetic and they resist change.

Ros T, Grade 11

The place for students with long, short, or no hair is in the classroom. The place for educators who like to tell people how to cut hair is in barber college.

Toronto Globe and Mail

The New York City Student Code

The New York City Board of Education, in November 1969, decided that the rights and responsibilities of the city's 275,000 high school students needed clarification. It therefore proposed a Code for Students. Some principals think its provisions are too liberal, and some militant students think they're too restrictive. Here, briefly, are the proposals:

• "Figurehead" student governments will be replaced by democratically elected governments with power to allocate money for student activities. Student representatives will meet, at least once a month, with the principal to discuss school policies, and will take part in decision-making on such issues as curriculum and discipline. A parent-student-faculty council will consult regularly with the principal, too.

• Student publications will be generally free of censorship, and will be permitted to express freely the policies and judgment of the student editors. They will, however, be obliged to observe standards of "responsible journalism"—which means avoiding libel, obscenity, and defamation of character.

• Students will have the right to wear buttons and badges, form political organizations, "including those that champion unpopular causes," and distribute literature. Such political activities, however, must not interfere with the regular school program.

• Unless dress is dangerous or so distracting that it interferes with education, students may wear whatever they like.

• A student will be entitled to a hearing and "due process" if he is suspended for more than five days.

14. Create a role-playing situation in which your class is divided in two. One half assumes the role of administrators and parents; the other plays the role of students interested in liberalizing school policy. (Ask your own school administrators to moderate.)

15a. Are these rules too liberal or too restrictive?

b. Will they be helpful to the process of education?

Both sides in this school argument are a bunch of spoiled ninnies. If they would both grow up, and stop babbling about the purposes of education, and students' rights and all that d--- nonsense, then they could get down to the business of education.

school janitor

THINK

(a) Resolved: That most protest in the schools is carried out by egotistical individuals who cannot adjust to the system themselves and, in their arrogance, wish to carry everyone else with them.

(b) Resolved: That, since man is inherently lazy, without discipline, restrictions and prodding, he and his civilization will deteriorate to nothing.

(c) Resolved: That schools are institutions where female values predominate and male patterns of behaviour are discouraged.

(d) Resolved: That free-enterprise schools are the answer to the current dilemma in education.

(e) List in order of importance, ten qualities of a good teacher. Compare the lists of various students for the predominant characteristics.

(f) "Without goals, teenagers will not work; and these goals must be provided by adults who are sufficiently experienced to know what those goals can realistically be." To what extent is that statement true?

(g) What is the difference between education and training?

(h) Is there a danger that our society may become overeducated?

11. POLLUTION

Man was the last to come to the Earth.
He shall be the first to leave it.

ECO-CATASTROPHE

(Dr. Paul Erlich, a prominent ecologist and professor of biology at Stanford University, published this scenario in the September 1969 issue of Ramparts Magazine.*)*

The end of the ocean came late in the summer of 1979, and it came even more rapidly than the biologists had expected. There had been signs for more than a decade, commencing with the discovery in 1968 that DDT slows down photosynthesis in marine plant life. It was announced in a short paper in the technical journal, Science, but to ecologists it smacked of doomsday. They knew that all life in the sea depends on photosynthesis, the chemical process by which green plants bind the sun's energy and make it available to living things. And they knew that DDT and similar chlorinated hydrocarbons had polluted the entire surface of the earth, including the sea.

But that was only the first of many signs. There had been the final gasp of the whaling industry in 1973, and the end of the Peruvian anchovy fishery in 1975. Indeed, a score of other fisheries had disappeared quietly from over-exploitation and various eco-catastrophes by 1977. The term "eco-catastrophe" was coined by a California ecologist in 1969 to describe the most spectacular of man's attacks on the system which sustain his life. He drew his inspiration from the Santa Barbara offshore oil disaster of that year, and from the news which spread among naturalists that virtually all of the Golden State's seashore bird life was doomed because of chlorinated hydrocarbon interference with its reproduction. Eco-catastrophes in the sea became increasingly common in the early 1970's. Mysterious "blooms" of previously rare micro-organisms began to appear in offshore waters. Red tides — killer outbreaks of a minute single-celled plant — returned to the Florida Gulf coast and were sometimes accompanied by tides of other exotic hues.

It was clear by 1975 that the entire ecology of the ocean was changing. A few types of phytoplankton were becoming resistant to chlorinated hydrocarbons and were gaining the upper hand. Changes in the phytoplankton community led inevitably to changes in the community of zooplankton, the tiny animals which eat the phytoplankton. These changes were passed on up the chains of life in the ocean to the herring, plaice, cod and tuna. As the diversity of life in the ocean diminished, its stability also decreased.

Other changes had taken place by 1975. Most ocean fishes that returned to fresh water to breed, like the salmon, had become extinct, their breeding streams so dammed up and polluted that their powerful homing instinct only resulted in suicide. Many fishes and shellfishes that bred in restricted areas along the coasts followed them as onshore pollution escalated.

By 1977 the animal yield of fish from the sea was down to 30 million metric tons, less than one-half the per capita catch of a decade earlier. This helped malnutrition to escalate sharply in a world where an estimated 50 million people per year were already dying of starvation. The United Nations attempted to get all chlorinated hydrocarbon insecticides banned on a worldwide basis, but the move was defeated by the United States. This opposition was generated primarily by the American petrochemical industry, operating hand in glove with its subsidiary, the United States Department of Agriculture. Together they persuaded the government to oppose the U.N. move — which was not difficult since most Americans believed that Russia and China were more in need of fish products than was the United States. The United Nations also attempted to get fishing nations to adopt strict and enforced catch limits to preserve dwindling stocks. This move was blocked by Russia, who, with the most modern electronic equipment, was in the best position to glean what was left in the sea. It was, curiously, on the very day in 1977 when the Soviet Union announced its refusal that another ominous article appeared in Science. It announced that incident solar radiation had been so reduced by worldwide air pollution that serious effects on the world's vegetation could be expected.

The Buffalo River, a tributary of Lake Erie, has been declared a fire hazard because of oil dumping.

Apparently it was a combination of ecosystem destabilization, sunlight reduction, and a rapid escalation in chlorinated hydrocarbon pollution from massive Thanodrin applications which triggered the ultimate catastrophe. Seventeen huge Soviet-financed Thanodrin plants were operating in underdeveloped countries by 1978. They had been part of a massive Russian "aid offensive" designed to fill the gap caused by the collapse of America's ballyhooed "Green Revolution."

It became apparent in the early '70s that the "Green Revolution" was more talk than substance. Distribution of high yield "miracle" grain seeds had caused temporary local spurts in agricultural production. Simultaneously, excellent weather had produced record harvests. The combination permitted bureaucrats, especially in the United States Department of Agriculture and the Agency for International Development (AID), to reverse their previous pessimism and indulge in an outburst of optimistic propaganda about staving off famine. They raved about the approaching transformation of agriculture in the underdeveloped countries (UDCs). The reason for the propaganda reversal was never made clear. Most historians agree that a combination of utter ignorance of ecology, a desire to justify past errors, and pressure from agro-industry (which was eager to sell pesticides, fertilizers, and farm machinery to the UDCs and agencies helping the UDCs) was behind the campaign. Whatever the motivation, the results were clear. Many concerned people, lacking the expertise to see through the Green Revolution drivel, relaxed. The population-food crisis was "solved."

But reality was not long in showing itself. Local famine persisted in northern India even after good weather brought an end to the ghastly Bihar famine of the mid-'60s. East Pakistan was next, followed by a resurgence of general famine in northern India. Other foci of famine rapidly developed in Indonesia, the Philippines, Malawi, the Congo, Egypt, Colombia, Ecuador, Honduras, the Dominican Republic, and Mexico.

Everywhere hard realities destroyed the illusion of the Green Revolution. Yields dropped as the progressive farmers who had first accepted the new seeds found that their higher yields brought lower prices — effective demand (hunger plus cash) was not sufficient in poor countries to keep prices up. Less progressive farmers, observing this, refused to make the extra effort required to cultivate the "miracle" grains. Transport systems proved inadequate to bring the necessary fertilizer to the fields where the new and extremely fertilizer-sensitive grains were being grown. The same systems were also inadequate to move produce to markets. Fertilizer plants were not built fast enough, and most of the underdeveloped countries could not scrape together funds to purchase supplies, even on concessional terms. Finally, the inevitable happened, and pests began to reduce yields in even the most carefully cultivated fields. Among the first were the famous "miracle rats" which invaded Philippine "miracle rice" fields early in 1969. They were quickly followed by many insects and viruses, thriving on the relatively pest-susceptible new grains, encouraged by the vast and dense plantings, and rapidly acquiring resistance to the chemicals used against them. As chaos spread until even the most obtuse agriculturists and economists realized that the Green Revolution had turned brown, the Russians stepped in.

In retrospect it seems incredible that the Russians, with the American mistakes known to them, could launch an even more incompetent program of aid to the underdeveloped world. Indeed, in the early 1970's there were cynics in the United States who claimed that outdoing the stupidity of American foreign aid would be physically impossible. Those critics were, however, obviously unaware that the Russians had been busily destroying their own environment for many years. The virtual disappearance of sturgeon from Russian rivers caused a great shortage of caviar by 1970. A standard joke among Russian scientists at that time was that they had created an artificial caviar which was indistinguishable from the real thing — except by taste. At any rate the Soviet Union, observing with interest the progressive deterioration of relations between the UDCs and the United States, came up with a solution. It had recently developed what it claimed was the ideal insecticide, a highly lethal chlorinated hydrocarbon

complexed with a special agent for penetrating the external skeletal armor of insects. Announcing that the new pesticide, called Thanodrin, would truly produce a Green Revolution, the Soviets entered into negotiations with various UDCs for the construction of massive Thanodrin factories. The USSR would bear all the costs; all it wanted in return were certain trade and military concessions.

It is interesting now, with the perspective of years, to examine in some detail the reasons why the UDCs welcomed the Thanodrin plan with such open arms. Government officials in these countries ignored the protests of their own scientists that Thanodrin would not solve the problems which plagued them. The governments now knew that the basic cause of their problems was overpopulation, and that these problems had been exacerbated by the dullness, daydreaming, and cupidity endemic to all governments. They knew that only population control and limited development aimed primarily at agriculture could have spared them the horrors they now faced. They knew it, but they were not about to admit it. How much easier it was simply to accuse the Americans of failing to give them proper aid; how much simpler to accept the Russian panacea.

And then there was the general worsening of relations between the United States and the UDCs. Many things had contributed to this. The situation in America in the first half of the 1970's deserves our close scrutiny. Being more dependent on imports for raw materials than the Soviet Union, the United States had, in the early 1970's, adopted more and more heavy-handed policies in order to insure continuing supplies. Military adventures in Asia and Latin America had further lessened the international credibility of the United States as a great defender of freedom — an image which had begun to deteriorate rapidly during the pointless and fruitless Viet-Nam conflict. At home, acceptance of the carefully manufactured image lessened dramatically, as even the more romantic and chauvinistic citizens began to understand the role of the military and the industrial system in what John Kenneth Galbraith had aptly named "The New Industrial State."

At home in the USA the early '70s were traumatic times. Racial violence grew and the habitability of the cities diminished, as nothing substantial was done to ameliorate either racial inequities or urban blight. Welfare rolls grew as automation and general technological progress forced more and more people into the category of "unemployable." Simultaneously a taxpayers' revolt occurred. Although there was not enough money to build the schools, roads, water systems, sewage systems, jails, hospitals, urban transit lines, and all the other amenities needed to support a burgeoning population, Americans refused to tax themselves more heavily. Starting in Youngstown, Ohio in 1969 and followed closely by Richmond, California, community after community was forced to close its schools or curtail educational operations for lack of funds. Water supplies, already marginal in quality and quantity in many places by 1970, deteriorated quickly. Water rationing occurred in 1723 municipalities in the summer of 1974, and hepatitis and epidemic dystentery rates climbed about 500 per cent between 1970-1974.

In 1970 the Ontario Federation of Agriculture urged its members to withhold their education taxes on the premise that too much was being spent on education.

City Hall at 8:15. This photo was taken from the 54th floor of the Toronto Dominion Centre one particularly smoggy morning.

City Hall at 11:15. This photo was taken from the same spot with the same camera using the same setting. The smog has lifted slightly and most of the haze has been dispersed by the rising temperature and a slight breeze that has come up.

Air pollution continued to be the most obvious manifestation of environmental deterioration. It was, by 1972, quite literally in the eyes of all Americans. The year 1973 saw not only the New York and Los Angeles smog disasters, but also the publication of the Surgeon General's massive report on air pollution and health. The public had been partially prepared for the worst by the publicity given to the U.N. pollution conference held in 1972. Deaths in the late '60s caused by smog were well known to scientists, but the public had ignored them because they mostly involved the early demise of the old and sick rather than people dropping dead on the freeways. But suddenly our citizens were faced with nearly 200,000 corpses and massive documentation that they could be the next to die from respiratory disease. They were not ready for that scale of disaster. After all, the U.N. conference had not predicted that accumulated air pollution would make the planet uninhabitable until almost 1990. The population was terrorized as TV screens became filled with scenes of horror from the disaster areas. Especially vivid was NBC's coverage of hundreds of unattended people choking out their lives outside of New York's hospitals. Terms like nitrogen oxide, acute bronchitis and cardiac arrest began to have real meaning for most Americans.

The ultimate horror was the announcement that chlorinated hydrocarbons were now a major constituent of air pollution in all American cities. Autopsies of smog disaster victims revealed an average chlorinated hydrocarbon load in fatty tissue equivalent to 26 parts per million of DDT. In October, 1973, the Department of Health, Education and Welfare announced studies which showed unequivocally that increasing death rates from hypertension, cirrhosis of the liver, liver cancer and a series of other diseases had resulted from the chlorinated hydrocarbon load. They estimated that Americans born since 1946 (when DDT usage began) now had a life expectancy of only 49 years, and predicted that if current patterns continued, this expectancy would reach 42 years by 1980, when it might level out. Plunging insurance stocks triggered a stock market panic. The president of Velsicol, Inc., a major pesticide producer, went on television to "publicly eat a teaspoonful of DDT" (it was really powdered milk) and announce that HEW had been infiltrated by Communists. Other giants of the petro-chemical industry, attempting to dispute the indisputable evidence, launched a massive pressure campaign on Congress to force HEW to "get out of agriculture's business." They were aided by the agro-chemical journals, which had decades of experience in misleading the public about the benefits and dangers of pesticides. But by now the public realized that it had been duped. The Nobel Prize for medicine and physiology was given to Drs. J. L. Radomski and W. B. Deichmann, who in the late 1960's had pioneered in the documentation of the long-term lethal effects of chlorinated hydrocarbons. A Presidential Commission with unimpeachable credentials directly accused the agro-chemical complex of "condemning many millions of Americans to an early death." The year 1973 was the year in which Americans finally came to understand the direct threat to their existence posed by environmental deterioration.

In downtown Chicago, polar bears in the city zoo suffer from emphysema and lung cancer.

*   *   *

The breast milk of many North American mothers now contains .2 parts per million of D.D.T., four times the safe level the U.S. gov't. allows in cow's milk for human consumption.

And 1973 was also the year in which most people finally comprehended the indirect threat. Even the president of Union Oil Company and several other industrialists publicly stated their concern over the reduction of bird populations which had resulted from pollution by DDT and other chlorinated hydrocarbons. Insect populations boomed because they were resistant to most pesticides and had been freed, by the incompetent use of those pesticides, from most of their natural enemies. Rodents swarmed over crops, multiplying rapidly in the absence of predatory birds. The effect of pests on the wheat crop was especially disastrous in the summer of 1973, since that was also the year of the great drought. Most of us can remember the shock which greeted the announcement by atmospheric physicists that the shift of the jet stream which had caused the drought was probably permanent. It signalled the birth of the Midwestern desert. Man's air-polluting activities had by then caused gross changes in climatic patterns. The news, of course, played hell with commodity and stock markets. Food prices skyrocketed, as savings were poured into hoarded canned goods. Official assurances that food supplies would remain ample fell on deaf ears, and even the government showed signs of nervousness when California migrant field workers went out on strike again in protest against the continued use of pesticides by growers. The strike burgeoned into farm burning and riots. The workers, calling themselves "The Walking Dead," demanded immediate compensation for their shortened lives, and crash research programs to attempt to lengthen them.

It was in the same speech in which President Edward Kennedy, after much delay, finally declared a national emergency and called out the National Guard to harvest California's crops, that the first mention of population control was made. Kennedy pointed out that the United States would no longer be able to offer any food aid to other nations and was likely to suffer food shortages herself. He suggested that, in view of the manifest failure of the Green Revolution, the only hope of the UDCs lay in population control. His statement, you will recall, created an uproar in the underdeveloped countries. Newspaper editorials accused the United States of wishing to prevent small countries from becoming large nations and thus threatening American hegemony. Politicians asserted that President Kennedy was a "creature of the giant drug combine" that wished to shove its pills down every woman's throat.

Among Americans, religious opposition to population control was very slight. Industry in general also backed the idea. Increasing poverty in the UDCs was both destroying markets and threatening supplies of raw materials. The seriousness of the raw material situation had been brought home during the Congressional Hard Resources hearings in 1971. The exposure of the ignorance of the cornucopian economists had been quite a spectacle — a spectacle brought into virtually every American's home in living color. Few would forget the distinguished geologist from the University of California who suggested that economists be legally required to learn at least the most elementary facts of geology. Fewer still would forget that an equally distinguished Harvard economist added that they might be required to learn some economics, too. The overall message was clear: America's resource situation was bad and bound to get worse. The hearings had led to a bill requiring the Departments of State Interior, and Commerce to set up a joint resource procurement council with the express purpose of "insuring that proper consideration of American resource needs be an integral part of American foreign policy."

Suddenly the United States discovered that it had a national consensus: population control was the only possible salvation of the underdeveloped world. But that same consensus led to heated debate. How could the UDCs be persuaded to limit their populations, and should not the United States lead the way by limiting its own? Members of the intellectual community wanted America to set an example. They pointed out that the United States was in the midst of a new baby boom: her birth rate, well over 20 per thousand per year, and her growth rate of over one per cent per annum were among the very highest of the developed countries. They detailed the deterioration of the American physical and pyschic environments, the growing health threats, the impending food shortages, and the insufficiency of funds for desperately needed public works. They contended that the nation was clearly unable or unwilling to properly care for the people it already had. What possible reason could there be, they queried, for adding any more? Besides, who would listen to requests by the United States for population control when that nation did not control her own profligate reproduction?

Those who opposed population controls for the U.S. were equally vociferous. The military-industrial complex, with its all-too-human mixture of ignorance and avarice, still saw strength and prosperity in numbers. Baby food magnates, already worried by the growing nitrate pollution of their products, saw their market disappearing. Steel manufacturers saw a decrease in aggregate demand and slippage for that holy of holies, the Gross National Product. And military men saw, in the growing population-food-environment crisis, a serious threat to their carefully nurtured Cold War. In the end, of course, economic arguments held sway, and in the "inalienable right of every American couple to determine the size of its family," a freedom invented for the occasion in the early '70s, was not compromised.

The population control bill, which was passed by Congress early in 1974, was quite a document, nevertheless. On the domestic front, it authorized an increase from 100 to 150 million dollars in funds for "family planning" activities. This was made possible by a general feeling in the country that the growing army on welfare needed family planning. But the gist of the bill was a series of measures designed to impress the need for population control on the UDCs. All American aid to countries with overpopulation problems was required by law to consist in part of population control assistance. In order to receive any assistance each nation was required not only to accept the population control aid, but also to match it according to a complex formula. "Overpopulation" itself was defined by a formula based on U.N. statistics, and the UDCs were required not only to accept aid, but also to show progress in reducing birth rates. Every five years the status of the aid program for each nation was to be re-evaluated.

The reaction to the announcement of this program dwarfed the response to President Kennedy's speech. A coalition of UDCs attempted to get the U.N. General Assembly to condemn the United States as a "genetic aggressor." Most damaging of all to the American cause was the famous "25 Indians and a dog" speech by Mr. Shankarnarayan, Indian Ambassador to the U.N. Shankarnarayan pointed out that for several decades the United States, with less than six per cent of the people of the world had consumed roughly 50 per cent of the raw materials used every year. He described vividly America's contribution to worldwide environmental deterioration, and he scathingly denounced the miserly record of United States foreign aid as "unworthy of a fourth-rate power, let alone the most powerful nation on earth."

It was the climax of his speech, however, which most historians claim once and for all destroyed the image of the United States. Shankarnarayan informed the assembly that the average American family dog was fed more animal protein per week than the average Indian got in a month. "How do you justify taking fish from protein-starved Peruvians and feeding them to your animals?" he asked. "I contend," he concluded, "that the birth of an American baby is a greater disaster for the world than that of 25 Indian babies." When the applause had died away, Mr. Sorensen, the American representative, made a speech which said essentially that "other countries look after their own self-interest, too." When the vote came, the United States was condemned.

This condemnation set the tone of U.S. relations at the time the Russian Thanodrin proposal was made. The proposal seemed to offer the masses in the UDCs an opportunity to save themselves and humiliate the United States at the same time;

and in human affairs, as we all know, biological realities could never interfere with such an opportunity. The scientists were silenced, the politicians said yes, the Thanodrin plants were built, and the results were what any beginning ecology student could have predicted. At first Thanodrin seemed to offer excellent control of many pests. True, there was a rash of human fatalities from improper use of the lethal chemical, but, as Russian technical advisors were prone to note, these were more than compensated for by increased yields. Thanodrin use skyrocketed throughout the underdeveloped world. The Mikoyan design group developed a dependable, cheap agricultural aircraft which the Soviets donated to the effort in large numbers. MIG sprayers became even more common in UDCs than MIG interceptors.

Then the troubles began. Insect strains with cuticles resistant to Thanodrin penetration began to appear. And as streams, rivers, fish culture ponds and onshore water became rich in Thanodrin, more fisheries began to disappear. Bird populations were decimated. The sequence of events was standard for broadcast use of a synthetic pesticide: a great success at first, followed by removal of natural enemies and development of resistance by the pest. Populations of crop-eating insects in areas treated with Thanodrin made steady comebacks and

"These damn signs will drive away our tourist trade."

> Quebec resort resident tearing down 'Unsafe for Swimming' signs.

soon became more abundant than ever. Yields plunged, while farmers in their desperation increased the Thanodrin dose and shortened the time between treatments. Death from Thanodrin poisoning became common. The first violent incident occurred in the Canete Valley of Peru, where farmers had suffered a similar chlorinated hydrocarbon disaster in the mid-'50s. A Russian advisor serving as an agricultural pilot was assaulted and killed by a mob of enraged farmers in January, 1978. Trouble spread rapidly during 1978, especially after the word got out that two years earlier Russia herself had banned the use of Thanodrin at home because of its serious effects on ecological systems. Suddenly Russia, and not the United States, was the *bête noir* in the UDCs. "Thanodrin parties" became epidemic, with farmers, in their ignorance, dumping carloads of Thanodrin concentrate into the sea. Russian advisors fled, and four of the Thanodrin plants were leveled to the ground. Destruction of the plants in Rio and Calcutta led to hundreds of thousands of gallons of Thanodrin concentrate being dumped directly into the sea.

Mr. Shankarnarayan again rose to address the U.N., but this time it was Mr. Potemkin, representative of the Soviet Union, who was on the hot seat. Mr. Potemkin heard his nation described as the greatest mass killer of all time as Shankarnarayan predicted at least 30 million deaths from crop failures due to overdependence on Thanodrin. Russia was accused of "chemical aggression," and the General Assembly, after a weak reply by Potemkin, passed a vote of censure.

It was in January, 1979, that huge blooms of a previously unknown variety of diatom were reported off the coast of Peru. The blooms were accompanied by a massive die-off of sea life and of the pathetic remainder of the birds which had once feasted on the anchovies of the area. Almost immediately another huge bloom was reported in the Indian ocean, centering around the Seychelles, and then a third in the South Atlantic off the African coast. Both of these were accompanied by spectacular die-offs of marine animals. Even more ominous were growing reports of fish and bird kills at oceanic points where there were no spectacular blooms. Biologists were soon able to explain the phenomena: the diatom had evolved an enzyme which broke down Thanodrin; that enzyme also produced a breakdown product which interfered with the transmission of nerve impulses, and was therefore lethal to animals. Unfortunately, the biologists could suggest no way of repressing the poisonous diatom bloom in time. By September 1979, all important animal life in the sea was extinct. Large areas of coastline had to be evacuated, as windrows of dead fish created a monumental stench.

But stench was the least of man's problems. Japan and China were faced with almost instant starvation from a total loss of the seafood on which they were so dependent. Both blamed Russia for their situation and demanded immediate mass shipments of food. Russia had none to send. On October 13 Chinese armies attacked Russia on a broad front. . . .

*   *   *

A pretty grim scenario. Unfortunately, we're a long way into it already. Everything mentioned as happening before 1970 has actually occurred; much of the rest is based on projections of trends already appearing. Evidence that pesticides have long-term lethal effects on human beings has started to accu-

---

As yet there is no way to decontaminate radioactive waste from nuclear power plants. Consequently it must be stored *perpetually*. One curie of strontium 90 will kill a human being. By 2000 A.D. the U.S. alone will have over six *billion* curies in storage.

---

mulate and recently Robert Finch, Secretary of the Department of Health, Education and Welfare expressed his extreme apprehension about the pesticide situation. Simultaneously the petrochemical industry continues its unconscionable poison-peddling. For instance, Shell Chemical has been carrying on a high-pressure campaign to sell the insecticide Azodrin to farmers as a killer of cotton pests. They continue their program even though they know that Azodrin is not only ineffective, but often *increases* the pest density. They've covered themselves nicely in an advertisement which states, "Even if an overpowering migration [sic] develops, the flexibility of Azodrin lets you regain control fast. Just increase the dosage according to label recommendations." It's a great game — get people to apply the poison and kill the natural enemies of the pests. Then blame the increased pests on "migration" and sell even more pesticide!

Right now fisheries are being wiped out by over-exploitation, made easy by modern electronic equipment. The companies producing the equipment know this. They even boast in advertising that only their equipment will keep fishermen in business until the final kill. Profits must obviously be maximized in the short run. Indeed, Western society is in the process of completing the rape and murder of the planet for economic gain. And, sadly, most of the rest of the world is eager for the opportunity to emulate our behavior. But the underdeveloped peoples will be denied that opportunity — the days of plunder are drawing inexorably to a close.

Most of the people who are going to die in the greatest cataclysm in the history of man have already been born. More than three and a half billion people already populate our moribund globe, and about half of them are hungry. Some 10 to 20 million will starve to death *this year*. In spite of this, the population of the earth will increase by 70 million souls in 1969. For mankind has artificially lowered the death rate of the human population, while in general birth rates have remained high. With the input side of the population system in high gear and the output side slowed down, our fragile planet has filled with people at an incredible rate. It took several million years for the population to reach a total of two billion people in 1930, while a *second two billion will have been added by 1975!* By that time some experts feel that food shortages will have escalated the present level of world hunger and starvation into famines of unbelievable proportions. Other experts, more optimistic, think the ultimate food-population collision will not occur until the decade of the 1980's. Of course more massive famine may be avoided if other events cause a prior rise in the human death rate.

Both worldwide plague and thermonuclear war are made more probable as population growth continues. These, along with famine, make up the trio of potential "death rate solutions" to the population problem — solutions in which the birth rate-death rate imbalance is redressed by a rise in the death rate rather than by a lowering of the birth rate. Make no mistake about it, *the imbalance will be redressed*. The shape of the population growth curve is one familiar to the biologist. It is the outbreak part of an outbreak-crash sequence. A population grows rapidly in the presence of abundant resources, finally runs out of food or some other necessity, and crashes to a low level or extinction. Man is not only running out of food, he is also destroying the life support systems of the Spaceship Earth. The situation was recently summarized very succinctly: "It is the top of the ninth inning. Man, always a threat at the plate, has been hitting Nature hard. It is important to remember, however, that NATURE BATS LAST."

"Is (heaven) more beautiful than the country of the musk-ox in summer when sometimes the mist blows over the lakes, and sometimes the water is blue, and the loons cry very often?"
(A Canadian Eskimo)

1a. Who is the villain in this scenario?

b. Dr. Erlich's essay has been accused of presenting its case in terms that are over-simplified — too black-white to be accurate. Can this accusation be substantiated?

2. The genre of science-fiction has been described as a prose treatment of a situation that could not happen in the world as we know it. Usually, however, the situation is based on some technical or pseudo-technical factors, whether human or extra-terrestrial in origin, thus giving the story a strong semblance of truth.

a) Is *Eco-Catastrophe!* science-fiction?

b) Is it fantasy?

c) Is the essay too technical to be effective?

d) Is it too horrible to be credible?

e) Is the definition of science-fiction adequate for the genre as you know it?

3. If you found *Eco-Catastrophe!* disturbing, precisely what disturbed you?

THINK

(a)　　　　Ecology　　　　　　　　birth-rate
　　　　　garbage　pollutants
　　　　　　　　　　　　　　　bio-degradable
　　　　　hydrocarbons

How important is the kind of vocabulary used to describe something? Is it time for a new vocabulary for pollution in order to awaken people to the seriousness of the problem? What words can you replace in the current pollution vocabulary in order to heighten the impact?

(b) What is the difference between "standard of living" and "quality of living"?

(c) Is there a danger in over-publicizing pollution?

(d) Some scientists have suggested that it is already too late to prevent ecological disaster, and that man would be wiser to turn his technological expertise toward developing artificial environments in which to live.

> *i.* Set up a committee (with sub-committees) to prepare the basic outlines of such a system. e.g. What kind of legal system would this type of living require? What kind of transportation? What living conditions? What kind of controls on the populace? Any sociological training? etc.?
>
> *ii.* Prepare speeches *to various kinds of audiences* explaining the advantages *to them* of such a system.
>
> *iii.* Select a committee to mount a campaign opposing this system.

(e) Devise a pollution-situation as Dr. Erlich has, and present your own version of an ecological disaster.
(Note: This is an example)
Jan. 14, 2062 A.D. Ever since the introduction of the jumbo-jets in 1969-70, a process has been taking place which no one was aware of until recently. Although science and the law combined forces to rid Earth of most of its pollution, little research was done on the effects of noise. Consequently, no one knew that the great jets produced a type of sound wave so intense that those people living near airports suffered subtle but permanent nerve damage which made them overwhelmingly aggressive. At the same time, these sound waves caused hormonal changes which made these people physically superior to other members of the human race. Within approximately 100 years it has become apparent that by the evolutionary process of natural selection, these people are becoming a master race....

(f) Assuming that there is intelligent life on another planet, what kind of report would an exploratory space crew send back to headquarters regarding Earth's environment?

12. PREJUDICE

Select Samaritan

by Robert Finch

We think we might adopt two children and
The problem is to know which kind we want.
Not Canadians. Refugees. But they can't
Be Jewish. A couple of Spaniards would be grand
If they were fair. My husband hates dark hair.
Afraid they are mostly dark in any case.
Germans would do, we don't care about race,
Except Chinese, must draw the line somewhere.

So would you let us know soon as you could
What sort's available? We have a car
And would be glad to come and look them over
Whatever time you say. Poles might be good,
Of the right type. Fussy? Perhaps we are
But any kids we take will be in clover.

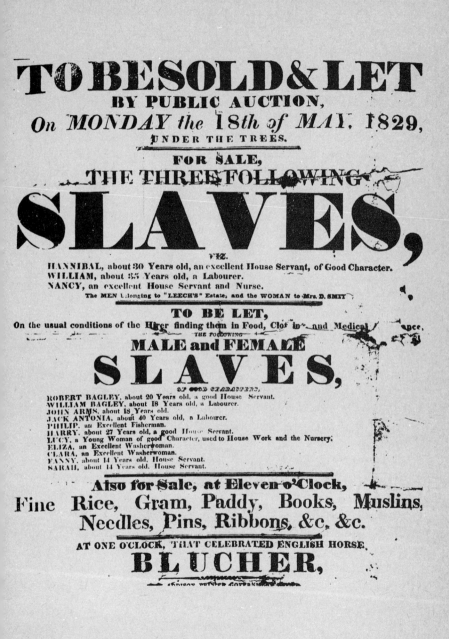

TO BE SOLD & LET

BY PUBLIC AUCTION,

On MONDAY the 18th of MAY, 1829,

UNDER THE TREES.

FOR SALE,

THE THREE FOLLOWING

SLAVES,

VIZ.

HANNIBAL, about 30 Years old, an excellent House Servant, of Good Character.

WILLIAM, about 35 Years old, a Labourer.

NANCY, an excellent House Servant and Nurse.

The MEN belonging to "LEECH'S" Estate; and the WOMAN to Mrs. D. SMIT

TO BE LET,

On the usual conditions of the Hirer finding them in Food, Clothing and Medical ance,

THE FOLLOWING

MALE and FEMALE

SLAVES,

OF GOOD CHARACTERS.

ROBERT BAGLEY, about 20 Years old, a good House Servant.

WILLIAM BAGLEY, about 18 Years old, a Labourer.

JOHN ARMS, about 18 Years old.

JACK ANTONIA, about 40 Years old, a Labourer.

PHILIP, an Excellent Fisherman.

HARRY, about 27 Years old, a good House Servant.

LUCY, a Young Woman of good Character, used to House Work and the Nursery.

ELIZA, an Excellent Washerwoman.

CLARA, an Excellent Washerwoman.

FANNY, about 14 Years old, House Servant.

SARAH, about 14 Years old, House Servant.

Also for Sale, at Eleven o'Clock,

Fine Rice, Gram, Paddy, Books, Muslins, Needles, Pins, Ribbons, &c. &c.

AT ONE O'CLOCK, THAT CELEBRATED ENGLISH HORSE,

BLUCHER,

What we've got to do is admit that the problem is *everybody's*. Once we do that we'll all start doing something about it.

Tom F. student (Grade 10)

1. Are you responsible when an Indian baby dies of starvation in Northern Canada? When a Métis is refused a job because he is a Métis? For what white people do to black people in Alabama?
2. After examining the poster very carefully, can you analyze in what ways it explains *today's* attitudes toward other races?

Is The Answer In "Black Power"?

In politics, Black Power meant independent action — Negro control of the political power of the black ghettos and its use to improve economic and social conditions. It could take the form of organizing a black political party or controlling the political machinery within the ghetto without the guidance or support of white politicians. Where predominantly Negro areas lacked Negroes in elective office, whether in the rural Black Belt of the South or in the urban centers, Black Power advocates sought the election of Negroes by voter registration campaigns, by getting out the vote, and by working for redrawing electoral districts. The basic belief was that only a well-organized and cohesive bloc of Negro voters could provide for the needs of the black masses. Even some Negro politicians allied to the major political parties adopted the term "Black Power" to describe their interest in the Negro vote.

In economic terms, Black Power meant creating independent, self-sufficient Negro business enterprise, not only by encouraging Negro entrepreneurs but also by forming Negro cooperatives in the ghettos and in the predominantly black rural counties of the South. In the area of education, Black Power called for local community control of the public schools in the black ghettos.

Throughout, the emphasis was on self-help, racial unity, and, among the most militant, retaliatory violence, the latter ranging from the legal right of self-defense to attempts to justify looting and arson in ghetto riots, guerrilla warfare and armed rebellion.

Phrases like "Black Power," "Black Consciousness," and "Black is Beautiful," enjoyed an extensive currency in the Negro community, even within the NAACP and among relatively conservative politicians, but particularly among young intellectuals and Afro-American student groups on predominantly white college campuses. Expressed in its most extreme form by small, often local, fringe groups, the Black Power ideology became associated with SNCC and CORE.

Generally regarded as the most militant among the important Negro protest organizations, they have developed different interpretations of the Black Power doctrine. SNCC calls for totally independent political action outside the established political parties, as with the Black Panther Party in Lowndes County, Ala.; rejects political alliances with other groups until Negroes have themselves built a substantial base of independent political power; applauds the idea of guerrilla warfare; and regards riots as rebellions.

CORE has been more flexible. Approving the SNCC strategy, it also advocates working within the Democratic Party; forming alliances with other groups and, while seeking to justify riots as the natural explosion of an oppressed people against intolerable conditions, advocates violence only in self-defense. Both groups favor cooperatives, but CORE has seemed more inclined toward job-training programs and developing a Negro entrepreneurial class, based upon the market within the black ghettos.

3. In your opinion, is Black Power a "left-wing" or a "right-wing" belief?
4a. What are the NAACP, CORE, SNCC?
  b. What are the basic differences in the way that SNCC and CORE interpret Black Power?
  c. Which of the two approaches (SNCC or CORE) will probably be more successful?
5. Is the phrase "Black Is Beautiful", prejudice?

Black Power: Two Views

A. from What We Want *by Stokely Carmichael (SNCC)*

Black power can be clearly defined for those who do not attach the fears of white America to their questions about it. We should begin with the basic fact that black Americans have two problems: they are poor and they are black. All other problems arise from this two-sided reality. . . .

Almost from its beginning, SNCC sought to address itself to both conditions with a program aimed at winning political power for impoverished Southern blacks. We have to begin with politics because black Americans are a propertyless people in a country where property is valued above all. We had to work for power, because this country does not function by morality, love, and nonviolence, but by power. Thus we determined to win political power, with the idea of moving on from there into activity that would have economic effects. With power, the masses could make or participate in making the decisions which govern their destinies, and thus create basic change in their day-to-day lives.

Where Negroes lack a majority, black power means proper representation and sharing of control. It means the creation of power bases from which black people can work to change statewide or nationwide patterns of oppression through pressure from strength instead of weakness. Politically, black power means what it has always meant to SNCC: the coming-together of black people to elect representatives and to force those representatives to speak to their needs. It does not mean merely putting black faces into office. A man or woman who is black and from the slums cannot be automatically expected to speak to the needs of black people. Most of the black politicians we see around the country today are not what SNCC means by black power. The power must be that of a community, and emanate from there.

B. from the testimony of Roy Wilkins (CORE) before a U.S. Senate Committee

QUESTION: What effect has the injection of the black power concept had upon the civil rights movement, in your opinion?
MR. WILKINS: Well, it has had some superficial effects. That is, it has caused some supersensitive people to withdraw, I mean white people.

It has also had an effect on some Negroes, in causing them to fail to analyze the situation and to react just as they think their power situation around them calls for them to react. But actually the black power thing has made Negroes think about their activity in America. Most of them don't like the black power formulation. It was unfortunate. It was hatched as a sort of football rally cry. It was a marching slogan down there in Mississippi, and you cannot handle the problems of 20 million citizens, who spent $27 billion a year as consumers, you cannot handle their destinies with a football slogan. It is too dangerous. It is too amateurish. It is too teenageish. It is too much like a student prank. You have to think about all the families that have investments, that have children, that own homes, that own businesses, that have relationships with white people, who have loans and mortgages at banks, who have jobs, who have hopes and ambitions. They do not want any antagonistic student slogan which has an ethnic tag to it.

6a. What does Stokely Carmichael recommend? What does Roy Wilkins recommend?
 b. What is each man's opinion of Black Power?
 c. What does each man think of his country?

Give them this day their daily bread.

Think of the last time that *you* were hungry. Really hungry. Was it because dinner was late? Or because you missed a lunch?

Can you imagine what it is to go through life never knowing what it is like *not* to be hungry? Subsisting day after day on a few greens around noon . . . and some pinto beans in the evening? Nothing more. Nothing different. And not even enough of that.

It sounds incredible. And it is incredible. Because it's taking place right now . . . in the midst of the good life so many of us are now living in America.

But walk down the back roads of most any Mississippi Delta town and you'll see tenant farmers, field hands, seasonal workers . . . and their children . . . with stomachs bloated, e y e s dulled, feet swollen, arms and legs matchstick thin.

The irony is that they aren't starving at a rate dramatic enough to arouse the indignation of the nation and the world. Otherwise something would have already been done.

One of the programs that is aiding many of these families is the federally sponsored Food Stamp Plan. Under this plan a needy family can convert a 50¢ food stamp into as much as $12.00 worth of food. The problem is getting that 50¢, because many families have *no* income at all.

The NAACP Special Contribution Fund has begun a nationwide drive to help thousands survive. If you can do with one less "dinner out" this month, the money can mean a month's supply of meat, milk, and bread for a family of five. Just $10.00 buys up to $240.00 in food stamps.

If you would like to contribute to this fund, please send your tax-deductible check, for as little or as much as you can, to the NAACP Mississippi Emergency Relief Fund.

Thank you. And may *your* next meal be a little more enjoyable.

7. The U.S. is the wealthiest country in the world. It has the largest gross national product in the world. It has the wealthiest people in the world. Do you think that *money* is the solution to the problem presented in the poster? Why or why not?

Desegregating Schools

Where racism exists anywhere in the world, one of the most sensitive issues has been segregation in the schools. The charge usually laid is that wherever non-white students predominate in North American schools, the education is inferior, for reasons ranging from inadequate budget to poor teaching. Whatever the causes, the charges are often borne out. In Canada for example, approximately 61 per cent of Indian children fail to reach Grade eight, (statistics: National Indian Brotherhood) whereas in some states in the U.S. the figures for black children are even worse.

In the late 1960's and early 1970's, the U.S. Federal government attempted a scheme of forced desegregation in the schools. Through a massive bussing program, students were to be transported to various schools in an area, according to a number-balance proportionate to the black-white population ratio. Black students were bussed out of the black community to white area schools, and white students were transported to what had been predominantly black schools. The reaction to this policy ranged all the way from quiet acceptance to outright rebellion.

8. What are some of the problems involved in *forcing* desegregation?
9. How would you react to being transported past the school near your home, to a strange part of the community?

In 1755 a male Indian's scalp brought a £40 bounty in New England. In 1756 the price jumped to £300.

The Way Of The Indian

from a radio documentary on the Canadian Broadcasting Corporation, 1961.

VOICE "The North American Indian had, within one generation of contact with the fur trader, become so utterly dependent on European firearms for hunting that the Company was fully justified in claiming that many thousand families of the natives, for want of the supply they annually received from us of guns, powder and shot wherewith they killed beaver, buffalo and several other beasts of that country, the flesh whereof is their food, would be starved before the next year. And Governor Jeremy left a tragic account of the starvation, cannibalism and infanticide caused by this lack of trading goods. For they have lost their skill with the bow since Europeans have supplied them with firearms."

CHIEF JOHN ALBANY And once the Indian learned to depend on firearms instead of the bow and arrow other problems arose. Warfare between the various tribes increased so much that the Hurons were all but wiped out. Fighting between Indians and white settlers became worse. And in the peaceful areas the Indian was able to kill all the game he liked. Before, he killed only enough for his needs. Now he killed all he could and the buffalo and the caribou became scarce. So it was the Indian's ability to adapt himself to the White Man's ways that resulted in us becoming completely dependent. We forgot how to make bows or tan hides. We adopted the White Man's dress. We traded with the settlers and bought our food instead of hunting, as in the old days.

ANNOUNCER There were other results just as serious. There was disease. We know by the number of medicine men and the many herbal remedies that there must have been plenty of sickness amongst the Indians, but it seems likely that many of the diseases common in Europe were unknown here. So the Indians had little resistance. And once smallpox appeared amongst the Montagnais of Quebec, in about 1635, it spread across Canada to the Rockies like a flood. Wave after wave of smallpox swept the country, and travellers told of finding tepees with every soul within lying dead. Tuberculosis and measles, too, were terrible killers among the Indian population, though medical science has reduced these till they're no longer a major problem. Then there was alcohol. The Indian had never discovered the art of making intoxicating drinks, though the Hurons did make a thin sour gruel from corn that had been allowed to ferment.

HUGH DEMPSEY I think it's rather interesting to note that at a very early period before the liquor was introduced to Western Canada, the Blackfoot Indian had no interest in drinking at all. And when liquor was first introduced it was given out free to the Indians to induce them to come to trade. In the beginning, the Blackfeet wouldn't even accept the liquor; they didn't want it, and it was only through the Hudson's Bay and Northwest companies almost forcing the Indians to take it as a means of getting control over them, that they did accept liquor. In the Blackfoot language the liquor is known as "Nabiochi", which means "White Man's Water".

ANNOUNCER That was Hugh Dempsey, the husband of a girl from the Blood Reserve. The diary of a trader gives us this picture of conditions in 1811:

VOICE "To see a houseful of drunken Indians consisting of men, women and children is a most unpleasant sight. For in that condition they often wrangle, pull each other by the hair, and fight. At some time ten or twelve of both sexes may be seen fighting each other promiscuously until at last they all fall on the floor, one upon the other. Some spilling rum out of a small kettle or dish which they hold in the hand, while others are throwing up what they have just drunk. To add to this uproar a number of children, some on their mothers' shoulders and others running about and taking hold of their clothes and constantly bawling, the older ones through fear that their parents may be stabbed or that some other misfortune may befall them in the fray. These shrieks of the children form a very unpleasant chorus to the brutal noise kept up by their drunken parents who are engaged in the squabble."

CHIEF JOHN ALBANY I don't know that this is any different from some white families I've seen. And it wasn't so common as you might think. But it was the start of the trouble that's been plaguing the Indian ever since. There are areas of the country where drinking is still a big problem. But we'll be telling you more about that later on. The more obvious results of the White Man's influence were: drunkenness, disease, war, declining population, and starvation in some areas after the White Man joined in hunting the buffalo. But something else began to happen. As the White Man and his culture spread westward, so did the decay of the native arts. First the Indian lost his native arts as he turned to the White Man's modern ways. Then the government took a hand.

DR. GILBERT MONTURE Now, when the White Man came, and especially after they put the Indian on the reserve, the wisdom of the old men in governing their tribal affairs was substituted for by the Indian Affairs administration. Administration and government by remote control if you wish to call it that. Too, the religion introduced was quite at variance with the religious rituals of the Indian peoples themselves. In fact, the Indian religions were frowned upon and perhaps even laughed away as being superstition, and as coming from the devil rather than from a beneficent Great Spirit in which all Indian tribes believe. And I have always felt that so sensitive is the primitive mind, which is almost childlike in its belief, that if you destroy one part of their society the rest tends to crumble and deteriorate.

ANNOUNCER The whole attitude of the White Man towards the Indian seemed to become one of contempt. This wasn't so true of the farmers and trappers who knew their Indian friends better, but the merchants and the army authorities and the government agents certainly gave the Indians the feeling they were looked down on. Mrs. Dave Crowchild feels she has every reason to feel bitter.

MRS. DAVE CROWCHILD Well, in olden days the agent never had no respect for us Indians. We used to go to his door, and most of the time he'd slam the door in our faces. They had no respect for us in those days. And even if our children were sick we couldn't take them to the hospital in town. They had to be looked after down here in some kind of a hospital that's on the reserve. I lost three boys just through carelessness, not getting the right medical attention. But you must try to understand, so I try to live different and to have no more hatred to white people.

CHIEF JOHN ALBANY It seemed as if our native cultures were being deliberately broken down. The Indian agents often knew little about us and cared less. It meant little to them that the old man knocking at their door might be a hereditary chief whose ancestry could be traced back for twenty generations. That he might have titles, and honours, and crests, and songs in his name. And it became a matter of government policy to civilize Indians by outlawing our pagan religions, our ceremonies, our songs. Even our language was discouraged. George Clutesy, a Nootka on the west coast of Vancouver Island, remembers those days well.

GEORGE CLUTESY We were not permitted to speak in our own language at all at any time during our stay in school. I know for a fact there are some of my own age group still living today who paid what we thought in them days was the extreme penalty. We were forbidden to speak in our own language, and if we were caught the first time we were reprimanded severely; if we were caught speaking in our own language the second time we were, what they called in them days, strapped. We were whipped. And if we were caught the third time, they took our only holidays away from us. And I think that done a great deal of harm. I think that one of the big suppressions that came in, came from the Chuch. I understand that they meant well, but I think they would have done better if they had asked the Indian: "What does it all mean?" They might have asked, for instance: "Do you believe in a God?" They would have learned that we did pray to a specific God. And I'm absolutely certain that it's the same God that we were taught later on. Had the Church asked us this, I think we would not have gone down so low. They had a great deal to do with the killing of our very spirit, with the wrenching from our very lives of the incentive to be our own selves.

ANNOUNCER This sounds very critical of the mission schools and of the Church's influence in general. You'll hear considerably more criticism from the Indians, too. You'll hear how the Indians were encouraged to destroy their totem poles by ignorant missionaries who thought they were pagan symbols.

In 1829 a Boethuk Indian slave girl died. She was the *last* surviving member of the Boethuk Indian tribe of Newfoundland, a tribe that was deliberately exterminated, first by another tribe, then by white settlers who were paid bounties for Indian scalps.

But you will also hear how the only contact with the White Man's world in some remote areas was through the selfless work of the missionary. The only schools, the only medical attention, were provided by the missions, and many of the Indians who have become nurses and doctors and teachers owe their success to the missions. One man who has dedicated his life to the Indians is Father Biladaut, principal of the Catholic residential school at Fort Qu'Appelle, Sask.

FATHER BILADAUT If we were sure, if we had the evidence, that we could do without the mission schools, we would. But first of all I might state that our school is a residential school, and naturally the first *milieu* or the first surroundings for education is the home. The parents have to be the first educators in the process of bringing up their children. Now, we know that there are many circumstances where the parents cannot or do not have the facilities to take over further responsibility for their children. They want them to be educated, but they do not know how. So they ask if we can take their children into our boarding schools because they want them to learn, they want them to be educated. And so I would say this is the purpose of our boarding schools. Segregated schools, I would say, would be in the same line again. A segregated school is where we have all our Indian children together, learning together, living together. And they are in a place where we think that the teachers and their supervisors, because of their experience, because of their understanding, will be able to help them more with their education — giving them more help than other people who maybe would not understand them as well.

CHIEF JOHN ALBANY We've been pretty critical of the White Mand and the effect he's had on us since he arrived in our country. But we should look at the other side of the picture too.

DR. GILBERT MONTURE In the early days of the Indian Affairs administration, and I'm speaking of the turn of the century, I would say that the Indian population had declined to approximately 130,000. I can recall on my own reservation that the incidence of tuberculosis was extremely high. I would say one out of five families had a relative or a member suffering from either advanced T.B. or incipient T.B. This was at Brantford Reserve. With the change in the thinking of government administration a program of health and medical care was instituted which has been really remarkable insofar as cutting down the incidence of disease and death among the Indians. So that today we have a population that is around 180,000—and this is one of the highest birth increases of any of the ethnic groups in Canada. So I think it is largely due to better health conditions and better food for the Indians. There's no doubt about it, the relief and welfare program of the government has done much to keep away starvation. But I do not think that this has given them the background of good nutrition that makes them good workers.

FATHER BILADAUT We must not forget that we white people think with centuries of civilization, if we may call it civilization, as a background. But our Indians here in Canada do not have much more than a hundred years or so. They have their own culture, their own ways of thinking, their own ways of living. And all at once the White Man came with his own ideas, his own culture, and pushed the Indians onto what they called reservations — pieces of land where they were gathered together, where they were secluded from the white men, who were afraid of the Indians and the Indians were afraid of the white men. Then all the Indians had developed a tribal attitude. The white people developed their own attitude. So much so that for quite a while they would not mix and they were led to live that way. Now all at once we say today: "Why don't they mix?" "Why should we not mix them together?" Well, this is something that has to be well understood by both parties, by the whites as well as by the Indians. And if they have a common understanding, then they will realize it themselves. Why should we not help one another as true brothers?

CHIEF JOHN ALBANY Whatever the reasons for the Indians living on reserves in the first place, the reserves have been responsible for saving us from extinction. We could have starved, we could have lost our land to the land grabbers. We've been safe on the reserve.

MRS. DAVE CROWCHILD No, I think we are better off on the reserve. Here on the reserve we seem to be away from a lot of bad things in life. You know, a lot of crimes and murders and everything going on outside. But it's not as bad as that here, and I think being on the reserve is what the Indians want. I've found out there's no harm in living on a reserve as long as we can work for ourselves and make our own livings. I think that would be all right.

CYPRIEN LAROQUE The younger generation today are living a lot better than in my young days. That is, they have a chance of making a good living by going out to work. There is more money now, and they have better things, better houses. They have a chance to get better houses. But in their manners they are not as good as the old Indians that I have known in my time.

ANNOUNCER An old timer, Cyprien Laroque, a Cree living in Alberta, can look back a long way. Yes, more money, better houses, better health, the secluded life, no responsibility. Certainly things are better than they were. Many on the reserves have cars instead of horses. The girls particularly can be very smartly dressed. But there's a price to pay for all this security.

HUGH DEMPSEY One of the big difficulties now is this attitude of the Indians of expecting everything to be done for them. They expect the government to look after them, look after their children, provide all their health and welfare facilities. And even if they are earning money they don't expect to have to pay any of this out for these various services. This is something that has developed over several generations of government paternalism, where the government has provided all of these things, and at the same time has taken away from the Indian the initiative to do things on his own and also the right to do various things on his own. It got to the point where the Indian felt that he didn't have a mind of his own, and expected the government to do these things right along, and each of the succeeding generations began to accept this way of life. Till now you have a complete paternalistic attitude and a feeling on the part of the government that these things now are expected, and the Indians are rather puzzled if they are turned loose and have to do them themselves.

CHIEF JOHN ALBANY This is one of the problems you have to face up to if you get to be chief of the band. Every scheme you want to organize, you've got two lots of people to sell it to. First the government, who want to control everything, and then the members of the band who often think the government should do it anyway. After a few generations of security on the reserve and government control, the Indians as a whole haven't got the ambition and the initiative they used to have. It makes you kind of bitter sometimes. Maybe we all ought to be like Leonard Crane, on the Sarcee Reserve, near Calgary, Alta.

LEONARD CRANE Well, I feel very sorry for the Indian agents because they're human beings like us. A lot of us Indians never realize that they are, you know, the same as we are. They've got families, a lot of them have family trouble, sick children, and they're under tremendous pressure. And I know they try. It's pretty hard to please everybody, and they're in a position where they have to get everybody happy, the guys in Ottawa and the fellows below them. And I try to work with them the best I can.

10a. List some of the important changes in Indian culture that were brought about by the white man.
  b. In your opinion, which of the changes are good? Which have been bad?
11. What reasoning, do you think, made government representatives, missionaries, and business people want to change the Indians' traditional beliefs and way of life? Why does change always seem to go in favour of the white man? Why does he not, rather, adopt the native culture that he finds?

12a. What problem does the Indian face today because of the reserves?
   b. How do reserves affect the existence of prejudice?

As long as Indian people are expected to become what they are not — white men — there is no basis on which they can meaningfully participate in Canadian society.

Harold Cardinal, President
Indian Assoc. of Alberta

Government May Take Action Against A Band Of Cree Indians

NORDEGG, Alta. (CP) — Even the wilderness areas of west-central Alberta may offer no refuge from the long arm of government for a breakaway band of Cree Indians.

Chief Robert Smallboy and about 150 followers left the Hobbema Indian reserve 50 miles south of Edmonton last August and moved westward to a wilderness area where they planned to return to the ways of their forebears and forsake what they considered inhumane aspects of white civilization.

Between 75 and 100 of the original group endured the winter on the Kootenay plains 40 miles southwest of here and 170 miles southwest of Edmonton. This week they are setting up their summer camp a few miles farther west.

But hanging over them is a possibility of government action against their continued location in the area.

The band is camped in the region of the White Goat Wilderness, and provincial regulations prohibit permanent settlement in the designated wilderness.

TO STUDY QUESTION

Dr. J. Donovan Ross, Alberta minister of lands and forests, said in an interview Wednesday the government is "not too concerned" about the location of Chief Smallboy's camp, but the question would be looked at shortly in case any action seemed necessary.

"They must know," Dr. Ross said, "that we need to give consideration to society as a whole, and not just to their concerns."

Meanwhile, members of the band, packing for the move to their summer camp, said they came through the winter in reasonable comfort despite the worst weather seen in the province for many years.

Tents were winterized with plywood and extra wood-burning heaters. There was plenty of wood and game, and the band members continued to receive their old age pensions, family allowances and reserve fund payments, including oil royalties.

Lazarus Roan, one of Chief Smallboy's senior lieutenants, said the band's future looks good.

He said 24 men obtained employment on clearing projects in connection with construction work on a new Calgary power dam on the North Saskatchewan River 20 miles from the camp.

According to the Canadian Department of Indian Affairs, Indians in Canada receive $25,000,000 annually in free medical care. According to the National Indian Brotherhood, the infant mortality rate of pre-school Indian children, is eight times the white rate.

Chief Smallboy, who at 70 years of age looks as though he might be in his 50s, met scepticism from many people in the Indian affairs department and at the Hobbema reserve when he led his followers west.

He had been trying for about 10 years prior to last August to win official approval for such a move.

He had travelled to Ottawa for a meeting with the minister of Indian affairs, talked often with local Indian affairs officials and journeyed several times to Edmonton to see provincial officials.

Finally he moved out without official approval, claiming he had been given a "run-around."

13. Present an argument in which you show either that Chief Smallboy has a solution to the Indians' difficulties, or that such a solution as he has devised, is impossible today.

Polish Anti-Semitism Sparks An Exodus To Denmark

COPENHAGEN — (Special) — "My son was brought up as a Christian. He never knew anything about Judaism until a year and-a-half ago."

The words came from a participant in one of the strangest chapters of the Jewish exodus from central Europe that began with Hitler's rise.

The man who played a leading role in Polish cultural life, is one of about 1,400 Polish Jews who have fled to Denmark in recent months to escape persecution.

Old-fashioned anti-Semitism, something many people thought long since disappeared from Europe, has played an important role in this new Exodus. But what makes it unusual, and in some respects even tragic, is that most of these new refugees do not view Israel as a second home.

Mrs. Hannah Kaufmann, a Danish volunteer worker with the refugees, explained why:

Many of these people were never aware of their Jewishness. They suddenly found themselves victims of somthing they didn't know existed."

Leo Fischer, a leader of Denmark's Jewish community, adds. "The majority of these people always thought of themselves as Communists. Those who wanted to go to Israel did so 10 years ago."

Of those who remained, Fischer said, many became active anti-Zionists as a result of years of anti-Israel propaganda in Poland.

Statistics bear this out. Only seven of the Polish Jews who have come to Denmark have elected to emigrate to the Jewish state.

Whatever their personal feelings, all these people had to formally opt for Zionism in order to get out of Poland. They had to renounce their Polish nationality and apply at the Dutch embassy in Warsaw for Israeli visas.

With these, they were allowed to leave on one-way travel papers identifying them as stateless persons, and without taking any money with them. About 11,000 have followed this procedure, but only about half have gone on to the Promised Land, according to Israel.

The price for an exit visa for the Polish Jews is about $230. This is about twice the average monthly income in Poland.

Two factors apparently lie behind this new wave of official anti-Semitism: The 1967 six-day Arab-Israeli war and the student and intellectual unrest that hit Poland in 1968.

It was then that Polish Communist leader Wladislaw Gomulka (whose wife is Jewish) publicly referred to Polish Jewry as a fifth column.

By itself, this probably would not have been enough to cause the flight of what is now reckoned at more than half the Jews that were left in Poland. But in 1968, prominent and lesser Jews were dismissed from their jobs. Then the Government offered all Zionists a chance to emigrate, and set last Sept. 1 as a cutoff date.

As a result, 900 Polish Jews arrived in Denmark in the months of October and November, and more went to Sweden, Italy, and elsewhere.

(Although the cutoff date did trigger the rush for visas and exit permits, it now appears the Polish regime will continue to issue them to any Jew willing to renounce his citizenship.)

The Danes were overwhelmed. They took over an ancient Canadian river boat called the St. Lawrence as an emergency reception centre. From there, the refugees have been distributed to 24 hotels in Copenhagen and 200 have found accommodation in the provinces.

Refugees is a funny word for these people. Most of them dress in moderately prosperous fashion, the women in fur hats and coats with matching fur trim. The girls wear mini-skirts and their hair long.

Although they were not allowed to take money out of Poland they could take all clothing and much other personal property, even some furniture.

In Denmark these refugees have found not only a haven but a host people whose hearts stretch out to all victims of persecution, particularly the Jews.

The Danes won world-wide admiration during World War II for getting all but 500 of their 6,000 Jewish population out from under the noses of the Nazi occupiers to sanctuary in Sweden.

They are extending the same protective concern to the new refugees, mainly through the Danish Refugee Council. This is a non-governmental organization set up in 1956 to handle refugees from the unsuccessful uprising in Hungary.

The Government here gives adult refugees three dollars a day plus free housing until they are established. Refugees who were pensioners in the old country get the Danish old age pension.

---

14. What are the reasons given for forcing the Jews out of Poland?
15a. Why has so much prejudice and discrimination been directed against Jews throughout history?
  b. What is the Danes' answer to this kind of prejudice?
  c. Why doesn't Canada or the U.S. imitate the Danes?

> I am the inferior of any man whose rights I
> trample underfoot. Men are not superior by rea-
> son of the accidents of race or color. They are
> superior who have the best heart — the best brain.
>
> Robert Green Ingersoll

Rhodesia

Other than the Union of South Africa, where apartheid policies have gained world-wide notoriety, the African country which has been most in the public eye is Rhodesia.

After unilaterally declaring her independence in 1965, Rhodesia set up what is essentially a white government even though the blacks outnumber whites, by 18 to 1. Much has been written about Rhodesia, and many people have advocated armed overthrow of the government. The following selection is part of a letter to the editor of *The Varsity* (University of Toronto campus newspaper) in response to an article condemning Rhodesia.

As an example of the unfair distortions and generalizations which frequently mark discussion of Rhodesia, I should like to deal in detail with some of the claims by Brian H. in last Friday's *Varsity:*

1) *"Education is completely segregated."* False. I attended a multi-racial school in Salisbury. However, government-run schools *are* segregated. One might not accept the reasons for this but they should have been presented. It is financially impossible for the Government to provide a full education for the whole school-age population of Rhodesia. The white tax-payers who provide the vast majority of governmental revenue demand

that their children not be educationally penalised because of this. Moreover it is felt that integration would have an adverse effect on the education of culturally more advanced white children (Rhodesians are not alone in thinking this way). I do not insist that these various reasons justify segregation, but they do put it in perspective. Finally the university *is* multi-racial. Perhaps Mr. H. does not consider this to be education.

2) *"Only 60% of African children get any education at all."* I do not know the source of this figure, but, assuming it is more reliable than some of Mr. H.'s other statements, I would point out that it compares very favourably with the rest of Africa. Also, since 1963, Rhodesia's expenditure on African education has risen 90%, high school enrollment has nearly tripled, and African enrollment at the university has more than doubled.

3) — *"The Law and Order Act . . . . . . has outlawed all African political parties."* False. Mr. H. means that specific nationalist parties have been banned for subversive activities and terrorism (largely directed against other Africans). The sweeping generalizations are typical of the falsifications in which he indulges. In fact an African party is represented in the legislature.

4) — *"All African political leaders . . . . . have been imprisoned or detained without trial."* False. Incorporated into this definitive statement of fact are Mr. H.'s unstated personal political prejudices, namely that the leader of the opposition and the thirteen other elected African MP's (who sit in the same legislature as the white MP's) are not leaders. He must also assume that the African chiefs and headmen who represent the bulk of the African population are not leaders either. These traditional leaders of African society, of course, are anathema to those of African political philosophy. One might ask, "When is an African not an African?" and be forced to conclude — only when he supports the government.

The net cummulative effect of the biased type of commentary we were offered last Friday is that most people have

come to accept a simplified version of a very complex problem — black is good, white is bad. In fact, in Africa the
difficulties are so great and so many that the question of who
rules serves only to distract from them. The substitution of
a minority black elite for a minority white elite brings no
advantage to the mass of the population. Indeed, quite the
opposite. Political inexperience and lack of technical skills
are likely to result in the political and economic instability
which have characterised and still do, the rest of Africa. What
does this imply? It implies hunger and starvation, violence
and insecurity — all in the name of human rights. Ask the
African in the street, not the politician in the limousine,
whether black government has made him feel better.

Probably the single most galling fact for Rhodesia's would-
be-liberators is the lack of popular support for their cause.
Rhodesia is one of the most internally peaceful countries in
the world. What fighting takes place is the result of guerilla
sorties from Zambia. The standard explanation for this is the
cry "police state". It does not stand up very well. As we are
so often told, the white population is less than 250,000. Subtract the women. Subtract the children. Subtract those needed
to keep the economy running. That does not leave very many
over to defend the borders against guerilla invasion and to
police millions of exploited and oppressed Africans, does it?

---

84 million people in India belong to the caste,
harijan, which means Untouchable. Peopled by the
children of inter-caste marriages, and the lowest
labourers, (streetcleaners, etc.), the Untouchables
form the lowest caste in the country, and are
treated like rejects from society.

It is not my intention to reverse the equation and pretend that the white is good while black is bad. There *is* racial prejudice in Rhodesia (and in Canada too). I suggest, however, that it is wrong to advocate destruction, slaughter of livestock, murder in the night, and ultimately war, when experience elsewhere in Africa teaches that the alleged benefits in terms of human dignity and welfare are unreal and when conditions in Rhodesia, compared with those elsewhere, do not merit such bloody solutions.

16a. What are some of the standard accusations made against Rhodesia?
 b. How does this letter make these accusations seem less serious?
17. Point out how this letter shows:
 a. that things are better in Rhodesia than what the world believes;
 b. that, in a sense, publicity about prejudice can be dangerous.
18. Do you feel that nations like Canada and the U.S. should advocate and support revolt among suppressed blacks in Rhodesia and South Africa?

THINK

(a) "Most of the prejudices that human beings develop, are learned as children. Sayings like 'Eeney, meeney, miney, mo, catch a nigger by the toe' help to convince children of a difference in racial quality."
Do you know of any remark, saying, or other prejudicial learning that you have experienced?

(b) "The goal of black people must not be to assimilate into middle class America. . . ." (Stokely Carmichael).
Do you agree with this position? (See also Harold Cardinal in this chapter.)

(c) "It is the working class, the blue collar class in our society that has most of the prejudice."
Is that an accurate statement?

(d) "Let's be honest about this. If I were in a war, and had to face somebody as I shot him, it'd be easier for me if he were another color, and the same thing would probably apply to him if the situation were turned around." (Keith G. Grade 9) Do you feel this way too?

(e) For investigation:

Try to discover some of the many areas of the world where prejudice exists.

(To start you — the Montagnards in Viet Nam

— problems in Belgium

(f) Prepare a report explaining how apartheid works in South Africa. (Make sure your report is strictly factual.) Have the class evaluate the system.

(g) Experiment with your own ability to control prejudice. Form four groups to do the following:

Group A

Group A prepares a description of an imaginary country with a prejudice problem. The problem must be fully described, with all its features fully outlined.

Group B

Group B plays the part of the government of that country. The government proposes a series of solutions to the problems that Group A has presented.

Groups C and D

Group B presents its solutions to Groups C and D. Group C represents the dominant race in the country, and Group D represents the race which is discriminated against. Both races explain their reactions to the solutions that the government recommends.

The Art of Listening

Being able to listen well, is vital not only to day-to-day activities, but also to sheer survival in the propaganda barrage of the modern world. Although research in the field is quite scanty, what details are available suggest that listening is one of the most poorly developed human skills.

The suggestions that follow, present a few ways to use *Prose of Relevance* for practice in the art of listening well.

Ken Weber

Note:
One of the most helpful techniques in discovering one's own bad listening habits is simply to discuss the reasons why people fail to listen. Every student in a class has certain listening prejudices such as *sounds* he may dislike, *subjects* he may dislike, *situations* in which he finds listening difficult. A general discussion of these personal listening difficulties brings the whole problem into a clearer focus.

Listening for the Whole Idea

(a) Tape record a brief class discussion on a particularly argumentative issue presented in *Prose of Relevance*. When the discussion is over, have some members of the class briefly summarize the stance taken by other students. Do not ask for detail, only the thesis or argument. The tape recorder usually resolves any disputes.

e.g. see "My Brother Was Deaf" in *Prose of Relevance 1*. Some of the questions invite everyone to take a stand, and voice an opinion which should be supported.

(b) Repeat (a), except this time try to prepare a written summary. Or, have someone (or a panel) present a summary to a student who has been out of the room.

(c) Read aloud a passage on a controversial topic. Then ask the students to describe the point of view, the emotional attitude of the writer, and some of the means by which the writer tries to *convince*.

Listening for Details

(a) Present a short talk to the class on a controversial subject. Include a few details that are either unrelated or only peripherally related. Have the class as a group, point out these details.

(b) Tape record a radio news broadcast that has little or no commentary. Record on the same day a broadcast that is full of commentary. Compare the results.

(c) Teacher, or student, reads a passage which expresses a point of view supported by considerable detail. (There are many examples in *Prose of Relevance 1* and *2*.)

Students can then attempt to recall as much detail as possible but the attempt should be based on specific questions asked by the teacher or other students. This can be done at first by pooling the memories and listening abilities of the whole class. Other techniques involve each student recalling details on his own, or true-false, and multiple choice tests.

Note: The object of this exercise should not be to develop ability to remember details, but to consider *why* people can remember certain details and not others. For example, a student should reflect on what there is about the detail that made him remember it; what in himself, and his own life, made him remember certain details.

The idea is that the student should not only think about his own ability to listen, but also think about the factors that affect his listening. Consequently, this technique should be varied:

i. Read the passage "cold" and follow with a true-false test.

ii. Conduct a discussion on the subject before reading the passage. Then read it. Test for listening.

"Filter-Listening" for Propaganda Techniques

The following methods have been outlined by the Institute For Propaganda Analysis (U.S.A.) as the predominant techniques of propaganda:

(a) Name Calling ("Commie", "Fascist", "racist", etc.)
(b) Glittering Generality (freedom-loving)
(c) Transfer (Giving the impression — whether it is true or not — that the speaker's cause is supported by various authorities such as church, government, experts, etc.)
(d) Testimonial (A speaker cites testimony from a well-known person, or, a well-known person such as a movie star may give testimony for something about which he is entirely ignorant.)
(e) Plain Folks (A speaker deliberately adopts the status and attitudes of a group to achieve his point)
(f) Card Stacking (Never revealing an opposite point of view — or admitting that one exists.)
(g) Band Wagon ("Look how many other people are doing it!")

The Institute does not include in its list, other techniques in oral persuasion such as: flattery; appeals to fear, hate, discontent; the creation of devils on whom to place blame; constant repetition; use of rumor and half-truths; etc.

Some Sources for Analyzing Persuasion

(a) *Prose of Relevance 2* (See particularly the section on "Law in a Democracy.")
(b) *Prose of Relevance 1* (See particularly the sample selections "Why Don't the Poor Work?" and "Marriage.")
   Note: Both (a) and (b) are given an extra dimension if someone in the class can give a persuasive oral presentation.
(c) If it is possible, attend a political figure's informal speech to a small group, especially if that political figure can also be seen on television or addressing a very large group.
(d) All the advertising media (See also "Facts Is Facts" in *Prose of Relevance 1*).